Mastering

APA Style

Mastering

APA Style

Student's Workbook and Training Guide

Harold Gelfand, Charles J. Walker, &
the American Psychological Association

American Psychological Association • *Washington, DC*

Published by
American Psychological Association
750 First Street, NE
Washington, DC 20002-4242
www.apa.org

First Printing—Oct. 2001
Second Printing—Dec. 2001
Third Printing—Mar. 2002
Fourth Printing—Dec. 2002
Fifth Printing—April 2004

Copies may be ordered from
APA Order Department
P.O. Box 92984
Washington, DC 20090-2984

Tel: (800) 374-2721, Direct: (202) 336-5510
Fax: (202) 336-5502, TDD/TTY: (202) 336-6123
Online: www.apa.org/books/
Email: order@apa.org

In the United Kingdom, Europe, Africa, and the Middle East, copies may be ordered from
American Psychological Association
3 Henrietta Street
Covent Garden, London
WC2E 8LU England

Typeset in Minion Display Regular and Memphis by EPS Group Inc., Easton, MD
Printer: Goodway Graphics, Springeld, VA
Cover Designer: Naylor Design, Washington, DC
Technical/Production Editor: Catherine Hudson

Library of Congress Cataloging-in-Publication Data
Gelfand, Harold.
    Mastering APA style : student's workbook and training guide / Harold
Gelfand, Charles J. Walker, & the American Psychological Association.
        p. cm.
    ISBN 1-55798-891-9 (acid-free paper)—ISBN 1-55798-890-0 (instructor's
guide)
    1. Psychology—Authorship—Study and teaching. 2. Social sciences—Authorship—
Study and teaching. 3. Psychological literature—Publishing—Study and teaching.
4. Social science literature—Publishing—Study and teaching. I. Walker, Charles J.,
1947– II. Title.
    BF76.8 .G452 2001
    808 .06615—dc21

                                                                2001053555

Mastering APA Style is the only instructional module prepared under the guidance of the American Psychological Association and designed to conform in every way with the style components set out in the Þfth edition of the *Publication Manual of the American Psychological Association*.

Printed in the United States of America

Contents

CHAPTER 1

The Purpose of *Mastering APA Style*

1

Imagine what writing would look like without style rules: Wee the peepul uv the Youknightd Staats in oardur too form ay moor purfekt yoonyun esstablish juctis ensur domestik tranqilettee provid four the commen deefenc promoat the genurol wellfair . . . oardan and establish thiss constitooshun . . .

What Is Style?

According to *Merriam-Webster's Collegiate Dictionary* (10th edition), *style* is "a convention with respect to spelling, punctuation, capitalization, and typographic arrangement and display followed in writing or printing" (p. 1169). When people first began to put words on paper, there were no customs or plans. Spelling was whimsical; punctuation had not been invented. There had been no need for such conventions. Listeners knew whether a speaker meant *where* or *wear* by the context of the speech. They knew when ideas were changing course because the speaker paused and drew breath. However, when people tried to read what others had written, confusion reigned. Imagine trying to read a page of text that has no commas, periods, or paragraph breaks; in which you cannot discern who is speaking because there are no quotation marks; and in which the same word may be spelled five different ways. The need for rules was immediately obvious, and style was born.

Who's on first?
Lessee hereby leases from lessor, and lessor leases to lessee, the property listed in the attached Schedule 1 and in any schedule made a part hereof by the parties hereto (herein called "equipment").

As soon as some uniformity had been achieved, it also became obvious that exceptions to the rules, or special rules, were needed as well. Chemists needed a universally understandable, shorthand way to refer to compounds and formulas. Lawyers needed a special way of communicating that eliminated ambiguity in phrasing the law. Scientists needed a way of reporting the results of their experiments. Researchers needed a way of citing the sources on which their ideas were founded. Each discipline had its own needs. The style used to write a will would not be useful for writing a research article. The style used for writing a research article would not be appropriate in an office memo.

> *Always credit your source:*
>
> *"My extensive research proves that women are smarter because they do not have to wear neckties to work"* (based on a chat with a chap at the train station).

It is important to realize that there is more than one "correct" style. The style conventions that you follow for your particular writing project will be those that best meet the needs of the discipline that you are writing for or about. Thus, journalists, lawyers, government officials, literary critics, and mathematicians follow style guides that were developed specifically to meet their needs and those of their intended audiences.

What Is APA Style, and Who Uses It?

Soon after psychology was established as an academic discipline, it was clear that a customized set of rules and conventions was needed. Theories of psychology are founded on research conducted with animals and humans. The ways in which research is conducted are standardized by the discipline. For example, there are well-defined procedures for using experimental controls, applying statistics, interpreting the validity of test scores, and so forth. When preparing written reports of such research, it is important that writers use the same conventions so that results and conclusions and the means of deriving them are universally understood.

Thus, APA style was originally devised specifically to meet the needs of people who write term papers, essays, master's theses, doctoral dissertations, journal articles, reports, or books in the behavioral and social sciences. APA style has also been widely acknowledged as a practical means to organize and communicate technical information in fields other than psychology (e.g., anthropology, sociology, management science), and many of these disciplines have adopted its use in their academic departments and professional organizations.

The handbook that lists the rules and conventions of APA style is the *Publication Manual of the American Psychological Association*. The fifth and most current edition was published in 2002. The *Publication Manual* is probably the most widely used style guide in the world. Hundreds of professional journals require their authors to use the *Publication Manual* as their style guide. Use of APA style is required by all psychology departments and by many other academic departments in U.S. colleges and universities. More than 200,000 copies of the *Publication Manual* are sold throughout the world each year.

Why Should You Use APA Style?

The reason for using any style guide is apparent: You want to be able to communicate your ideas clearly to others. Writing has two components: content and style. *Content* is what you say; *style* is how you say it. You may have great ideas, but if your manuscripts are poorly prepared (e.g., if you make numerous grammatical errors, are repetitive, fail to cite sources, present tables that are difficult to interpret), you lose credibility with the reader. If that reader is your instructor, he or she may think that you do not comprehend your subject matter.

If you are a student of psychology or a related discipline, you should use APA style because it will enable you to communicate in a way that is familiar to and accepted by the people for whom you are or will be writing (who number in the hundreds of thousands!). If lawyers ignored the style conventions used by their colleagues, their written work would probably be viewed with great skepticism (e.g., "When I kick the bucket, give all the junk in my basement to my friend Bill, but only if he promises not to sell anything at one of his yard sales"). If statisticians invented their own way of presenting probabilities and did not use the guidelines accepted by their field, readers would have great difficulty interpreting their numbers (e.g., "The phi delta chi probability is less than gamma magna probability"). Your discipline requires you to follow APA style—and for good reason.

Therefore, there are two fundamental reasons why you should use APA style: Following any style guide will enable you to communicate better, and following APA style is required in your discipline. What you may not realize is that many personal benefits will accrue to you as you use APA style. Set aside for a moment the idea that APA style is required, and consider what is in it for you:

• The *Publication Manual* is more than a list of rules and guidelines; it also contains sound advice on the craft of writing (chapters 1 and 2). Thus, APA style will help you to improve your writing skills not only for the courses in which it is required but also for any writing that you do.

• Having rules and guidelines readily available for troublesome or complicated issues such as formatting references or displaying statistics saves you time and trouble: You do not have to create ways of doing these things. Your time is freed up to concentrate on content.

• Often writer's block occurs because you cannot see how to arrange your information. Should you discuss each implication as you present each result, or should you present all of the results and then all of the implications? Should you introduce your paper by summarizing your conclusions or begin by describing your procedures and present your conclusions only at the end? There are myriad decisions to be made. The *Publication Manual* offers a ready-made outline that can help you organize your thoughts before you write and as you write.

• If you follow APA style guidelines correctly, your writing will be free of most of the mechanical errors that can distract your readers from the ideas—the content—that you are presenting. By showing respect for your readers, you gain their respect and their interest in your subject.

• The more you use APA style, the more mastery you will achieve. When you achieve mastery, you will have internalized good writing skills as well as knowledge of the basic style rules. Thus, in any subsequent writing you do, you will need to consult the *Publication Manual* less and less often and will approach any writing task with greater confidence and competence. In other words, the benefits continue to accrue beyond your first term paper.

• If you do plan to pursue graduate study or a professional career in psychology or a related discipline, you will probably be required to write for publication. Most publishers in your discipline require that you conform to APA style. Thus, by mastering APA style now, you help ensure your chances of success in graduate study or a professional career.

• From a purely academic standpoint, there is no question that by improving your writing skills —even only the mechanics—you will get better grades. By preparing your papers well you increase the likelihood that you convey what you know.

So you see, mastering APA style has many practical advantages beyond getting you through your first course that requires it. You will save time, improve your writing skills, write with greater ease and confidence, improve your chances of getting better grades, and—most important—equip yourself with a valuable skill that will continue to serve you in the future, regardless of what career course you choose.

How Will This Workbook Help You Learn APA Style?

Chances are that you are reading this book because you are required to learn APA style. It is quite natural for you to question this requirement. You may view it as an unwelcome demand on your time. You may wonder how you can be expected to learn APA style in addition to learning the subject matter of your course. If you are fairly certain that you will not go to graduate school, you may wonder why you have to learn all of these rules just to write a few papers. The preceding section should convince you that learning APA style will be beneficial for you regardless of whether you write only one paper for a required course or whether you go on to graduate school or a profession. Even if you are convinced that you need to learn APA style, how will you do it? How will you find the time? Will you have to memorize the entire *Publication Manual*?

If reading a copy of the *Publication Manual* is your only means of learning APA style, the task can seem daunting. There is a great deal of material to learn, and there are many small details to remember. Many of the guidelines seem arbitrary to you. Thus, it is difficult for you to understand why you should have to use them. For example, why does a paper have to be double-spaced? Why do references have to be put in alphabetical order? Why do you have to say *humankind* instead of *mankind*? As you gain experience, you will understand the practical reasons for style rules that are not so apparent at first. It is easier to learn anything if you understand its application.

You will discover that many style guidelines are intended to aid the reader. For example, double-spaced manuscripts are easier to read than single-spaced manuscripts, alphabetizing references makes it easier for readers to look them up, and using nonsexist language shows respect and sensitivity for your audience. Some style rules, such as some of the rules for numbers, are indeed arbitrary. Such style rules exist simply because consistency is preferable.

The trouble with learning APA style from the *Publication Manual* alone is that although examples of usage are given, the book does not offer you practice in applying rules to real-life situations. Remember that the *Publication Manual* is a reference book, not a how-to book. *Mastering APA Style* was designed to make learning APA style easy for you and to save you time. No, you will not have to memorize the entire *Publication Manual*. In fact, memorizing the guidelines will not enable you to master APA style. Mastery comes through practice. Think of using APA style as a skill or a tool rather than as a subject matter to be memorized. APA style is a means, not an end, a means of becoming your own writing critic or editor.

This user-friendly workbook is written in such a way that you may study on your own, at your own pace, without supervision. Individual instructors may offer you guidance, class time, or deadlines, all of which will only help you further. The workbook also teaches through practice (i.e., hands-on learning). The exercises and tests require you to apply APA style, not necessarily to prove that you have memorized it. Furthermore, you may not need to complete the entire workbook. The workbook is full of road markers (i.e., the sections of the *Publication Manual* to which a style point pertains is always cited) so that you can work on only those areas that you need to work on. Although this workbook is designed to teach you about APA stle, it will also inform you about psychology. The exercises draw on what has been done in a variety of areas within psychology. You will learn about theories, methods, research, and applications by many different psychologists representing diverse groups.

CHAPTER 2

How to Use the *Student's Workbook and Training Guide*

2

Organization of the Workbook

Take a moment to look at the table of contents for the *Student's Workbook and Training Guide.* Chapter 1, which you should have just read, describes the purpose of *Mastering APA Style* and describes what style is in general and what APA style is in particular. Perhaps most important, the chapter outlines the benefits that you will gain by mastering APA style. If you have any doubts about why you need to be able to use APA style or how this book will help you learn, chapter 1 should help you resolve them. In this chapter, the organization and content of the workbook are described in greater detail, and instructions are given for using the materials. It is essential to read chapter 2 to understand how to use the materials most efficiently.

As the table of contents shows, the learning materials are divided into two units: term paper writing (chapter 3) and research report writing (chapter 4). If you do not need to write reports of empirical research presently or in the near future, you need complete only the term paper unit. However, everyone, including those who will be writing research reports, should do the term paper unit because the basic principles it teaches are the foundation for the more technical principles taught in the research report unit. Within each unit, you will see that the learning materials are divided into four components:

- Familiarization Test
- Learning Exercises and Integrative Exercises
- Practice Test
- Review Exercises.

The learning, integrative, and review exercises are further subdivided by topic.

An important thing to know is that all of the answers to test and exercise items are in the workbook. The tests have answer keys, and the exercises consist of a draft version (the question) and a feedback version (the answer). You will not be left wondering whether you have correctly applied a style rule; there is no mystery. This feature of the workbook is explained more fully under "Instructions for Using the Workbook Materials" later in this chapter.

Using the *Publication Manual* With the Workbook

Now take a moment to leaf through the *Publication Manual.* You will notice that each chapter is subdivided into numbered sections. For example, in chapter 2, "Expressing Ideas and Reducing Bias in Language," you will find a subsection coded 2.01 ("Orderly Presentation of Ideas"). In the code 2.02, the number to the left of the decimal identifies the chapter number; the number to the right of the decimal identifies the section, which is also a specific point of style, or rule. These numbers simplify the process of finding style rules in the *Publication Manual.* The same numbering system is used in the *Student's Workbook and Training Guide* to assist you in locating the section of the *Publication Manual* pertinent to the style point you are studying. These numbers are referred to as "APA codes," and they are listed with each test and exercise item.

Buy a copy of the Publication Manual.
Always do the term paper unit first.
Always take the familiarization test before doing the learning exercises.

Where Should You Begin?

Be sure you have a copy of the *Publication Manual* (fifth edition) before you begin to use the workbook. You should definitely complete the term paper unit before doing the research report unit, even if you need to know APA style only for writing research reports. The reason is that the research report unit builds on the principles taught in the term paper unit. It is also strongly recommended that you take a familiarization test before doing the learning exercises. Doing so may save you significant time and effort because it will help you to identify particular style points that you have already mastered; thus, you may choose to skip the learning exercises pertaining to those points.

Although the order of the exercises corresponds roughly to the order of the sections of the *Publication Manual* indicated by APA codes, the workbook is designed for independent study and can be used flexibly. Unless your instructor makes specific assignments, you may complete the exercises in any order you find useful. To facilitate skipping around, each topic area is preceded by a brief synopsis of what style points the exercises for that section teach and how to complete them.

You may also wonder whether you should do all of the exercises in a section (e.g., exercises on punctuation) and then go back and look at the feedback version (the correct version of each exercise item) or whether you should do them one by one. Either way is fine. The same advice applies to consulting the *Publication Manual.* That is, you may want to consult the *Publication Manual* each time a question arises in your mind. Or you may read whole sections before or after doing the exercises. Whatever works for you!

Two approaches to doing learning exercises:

- *Do one exercise, jotting down changes or notes right on the workbook page. Then look at the feedback version and compare your work with the correct version. Consult the* Publication Manual *as questions arise. Go on to the next exercise.*
- *Do all of the exercises in a section, jotting down changes or notes right on the workbook page. Then review all of the feedback versions. Consult the* Publication Manual *at any time.*

Instructions for Using the Workbook Materials

There are several things you should know about the materials contained in *Mastering APA Style.* Understanding how the materials are written, arranged, and formatted before you begin working will make your task easier. These matters are explained in further detail later in this chapter.

- *Mastering APA Style* consists of two books: the *Instructor's Resource Guide* and the *Student's Workbook and Training Guide.* You need only the *Student's Workbook and Training Guide.* The *Instructor's Resource Guide* contains the mastery tests, the mastery test answer keys and answer sheets, and the complete test item pool. Your instructor will provide you with any mastery test, along with an answer sheet, that you may be asked to take.

- All test and exercise items cite APA codes, which indicate the sections of the *Publication Manual* that contain the style guidelines that pertain to the questions and exercises.

- The tests and exercises do not cover the *Publication Manual* comprehensively. They focus on chapters 1 through 5, which contain most of the editorial style guidelines.

- Test and exercise items are grouped by topic, and they are arranged to correspond approximately to the order of the *Publication Manual.*
- All test items have a multiple-choice answer mode. There are no yes−no, true−false, or essay questions per se.
- The tests consist of three styles of questions: complete statements or questions, incomplete statements, and unedited segments of manuscript.
- Some of the tests and exercises are designed to aid you in memorizing important aspects of APA style, whereas others are intended to help you learn how to use the *Publication Manual* itself or to look up infrequently used technical information.

There are three styles of questions in the tests:

- *Complete statements or questions, for which you choose the correct response.*

20. Which of the following examples should not be hyphenated?
    a. role-playing technique
    b. super-ordinate variable
    c. six-trial problem
    d. high-anxiety group
    e. all of the above

- *Incomplete statements, for which you choose the response that accurately completes the statement (i.e., fill in the blank).*

21. In titles of books and articles, initial letters are capitalized in
    a. major words when titles appear in regular text.
    b. words of four letters or more when titles appear in regular text.
    c. the second word in a hyphenated compound when titles appear in regular text.
    d. major words and words of four letters or more when titles appear in reference lists.
    e. all of the above except d.

- *Unedited segments of manuscripts, which you edit and then choose the response that reflects how you edited the text.*

11. Edit the following for the use of nonsexist language:

    It has been suggested that the major factor giving man a performance advantage over other primates on many cognitive tasks is that the tasks have been selected and administered by other men.

a. leave as is

b. It has been suggested that the major factor giving the species of man a performance advantage over other primates on many cognitive tasks is that the tasks have been selected and administered by men of the same species.

c. It has been suggested that the major factor giving human beings a performance advantage over other primates on many cognitive tasks is that the tasks have been selected and administered by other human beings.

d. It has been suggested that the major factor giving human beings (men or women) a performance advantage over other primates on many cognitive tasks is that the tasks have been selected and administered by other human beings.

Familiarization Tests

Taking the familiarization tests and reviewing your responses to them will help you to identify what you do know and do not know about APA style. The time you spend on the familiarization tests is time well spent. In the long run these tests will save you time because you will be able to focus your study efforts on only those topics that you need most to learn or master.

The tests consist of 40 numbered items, each followed by a series of possible responses identified by lowercase letters (e.g., a, b, c). Only one response is correct for each item. Two answer sheets for each test are located at the end of the tests. One is blank, so that you can write in your responses. The other contains the answers and the APA codes for each item. Read each test item, read the possible responses, and write in the letter of the response that you think is correct on the blank answer sheet. You may consult the *Publication Manual* at any time. You may find it useful to make a notation next to any test item that you found to be difficult.

When you have responded to all of the test items, check your work against the answer key and score your own test. To get an accurate assessment of how much you know, when you score your familiarization test, count only those questions you answered correctly without the aid of the *Publication Manual*. If the total number of incorrect answers plus looked-up answers is greater than 20% (i.e., 8 or more of a possible 40 answers), consider doing all of the learning exercises. While you are doing the exercises, pay special attention to those aspects of APA style that you are the least familiar with (i.e., read and practice those parts of the *Publication Manual* you missed on the test).

However, if you did well on the familiarization test (e.g., a score of 36 or better), you may save time by skipping the learning exercises. If you are doing this work as a requirement for a course, your instructor may choose to give you a mastery test; to prepare yourself for these tests, simply do the review exercises and take the practice test.

Even if you did well on the familiarization test, you may elect to go through all of the learning exercises and review exercises to strengthen your application skills. As was explained earlier, you may choose to do all of the exercises in sequence or to focus on those that deal with problem areas. For example, if the APA codes listed next to one of your incorrect responses on the test answer key are 1.03–1.05, you may want to find all of the exercises that list codes 1.03, 1.04, and 1.05 and complete those first.

Learning Exercises and Integrative Exercises

The correct version of each exercise, called the *feedback version*, always appears on the left-hand page. The incorrect version of each exercise, called the *draft version*, always appears on the right-hand page. Before beginning, it is recommended that you cover up the feedback version on the left-hand page. There are two types of exercises: learning exercises and integrative exercises. Learning exercises are brief excerpts of text that address one or two components of APA style. The component being targeted is shaded. Read the text and decide whether the text in the shaded area is correct or incorrect. Write corrections on the workbook page directly above the errors. By examining the feedback version of the exercise on the left-hand page, you can check the accuracy of your editing. The feedback version will either state "correct as is," or the correctly edited material will be shaded. An APA code and inventory number are given for each exercise; you should ignore the latter.

Sample Learning Exercise

Draft

The confederate, who was going to agree with the participant, always spoke up before the confederate, who was going to disagree with the participant.

APA CODE: 3.02 INDEX NUMBER: 05

Feedback

The confederate who was going to agree with the participant always spoke up before the confederate who was going to disagree with the participant.

APA CODE: 3.02 INDEX NUMBER: 05

Integrative exercises consist of a paragraph or page of text that you are instructed to edit. Style components are not targeted with shading, but you are directed to the general topic areas. Read the text carefully and edit it as you deem appropriate, writing in your changes on the draft version. On the feedback version of integrative exercises (again, always directly to your left) all essential corrections are shaded. One integrative exercise appears at the end of each topic section.

Sample Integrative Exercise

Draft: Reference Citations in Text

Holmes and Rahe (Holmes & Rahe, 1967) argued that change, especially major change, causes stress. Boyce, Jensen, Cassel, Collier, Smith, and Ramey (1977) found that stress mediated by life events reduces resistance to respiratory infections. Other researchers (Lazarus, 1980) have focused on the more mundane stresses, or "hassles," in daily life as predictors of illness and depression. The person's evaluation of the event, as much as the nature of the event itself, affects the degree to which an event is experienced as stressful (Lazarus, Speisman, Davison, & Mordkiff, 1964; Lazarus, 1966; Lazarus, 1968; Lazarus & Launier, 1978).

Numerous techniques have been developed to help people cope with stress. Progressive relaxation (e.g., Jacob, Kraemer and Agras, 1977) and biofeedback (e.g., Yates, 1980) have been used to control arousal. Jacob, Kraemer, and Agras found that progressive relaxation reduced high blood pressure. The critical role of cognitive appraisal in stress underlies stress management programs (Meichenbaum & Jaremko, 1983; Meichenbaum & Turk, 1982). Meichenbaum et al. (1982) had participants plan ahead and develop strategies for dealing with stressful situations.

APA CODES: 3.94–3.103   INDEX NUMBER: 01

Feedback: Reference Citations in Text

Holmes and Rahe (1967) argued that change, especially major change, causes stress. Boyce et al. (1977) found that stress mediated by life events reduces resistance to respiratory infections. Other researchers (Lazarus, 1980) have focused on the more mundane stresses, or "hassles," in daily life as predictors of illness and depression. The person's evaluation of the event, as much as the nature of the event itself, affects the degree to which an event is experienced as stressful (Lazarus, 1966, 1968; Lazarus & Launier, 1978; Lazarus, Speisman, Davison, & Mordkiff, 1964).

Numerous techniques have been developed to help people cope with stress. Progressive relaxation (e.g., Jacob, Kraemer, & Agras, 1977) and biofeedback (e.g., Yates, 1980) have been used to control arousal. Jacob et al. found that progressive relaxation reduced high blood pressure. The critical role of cognitive appraisal in stress underlies stress management programs (Meichenbaum & Jaremko, 1983; Meichenbaum & Turk, 1982). Meichenbaum and Turk had participants plan ahead and develop strategies for dealing with stressful situations.

APA CODES: 3.94–3.103   INDEX NUMBER: 01

Practice Tests

There are two practice tests in the workbook: one for the term paper unit and one for the research report unit. Practice tests are formatted identically to the familiarization tests, and you take these tests in the same manner. Answer sheets, one blank and one with answers, appear after each test. (See the earlier section, "Familiarization Tests.") Only the purpose of the practice tests differs. They are designed to provide feedback that you can use to

- assess your level of mastery after completing the learning exercises and integrative exercises,
- decide whether to study particular topics in the *Publication Manual* in more depth,
- decide whether to go on to the review exercises, or
- decide whether to take a mastery test.

Review Exercises

All review exercises are in the integrative format. You complete these exercises in the same manner as you did the earlier integrative exercises. Review exercises are designed to give you additional practice, to help you review style points you have already studied, and to further prepare you to take a mastery test. If you scored low on the practice test (80% or lower), you are urged to do these exercises. Similarly, if you have taken a mastery test but did not score 90% or higher, you may want to turn to these exercises before attempting another mastery test.

You should know that the exercises do not cover all of the material that is tested in the mastery tests. The reason for this is that some of the information in the *Publication Manual* is conceptual and cannot easily be made into concrete examples. However, we found that the conceptual material could easily be tested in multiple-choice questions.

Beyond the Workbook: Using Other Resources

The Role of Your Instructor

The role that an instructor assumes in teaching APA style and in using this training module will vary from instructor to instructor. Your instructor should define for you at the outset of the course what level of involvement he or she will have. The following are some of the most probable ways in which instructors may be involved in teaching APA style:

- Provide an overview of APA style and use of the workbook.
- Define goals and standards of achievement, that is, deadlines and criteria for demonstrating mastery.
- Provide class time for instruction, questions, or taking tests.
- Give feedback on performance on tests and exercises.
- Administer, score, and give feedback on mastery tests.
- Supply supplemental materials such as model manuscripts that use APA style correctly or incorrectly and tests or exercises that are different from those in your workbook. (Some of these supplemental materials are described more fully in the following sections.)

Mastery Tests

As we mentioned earlier, the *Instructor's Resource Guide* contains mastery tests that you may be called on to take. Mastery tests are the primary means by which your instructor can evaluate your knowledge of APA style and your readiness to prepare writing assignments. They are similar in structure and content to the familiarization and practice tests but contain different questions. Your instructor will score these tests; your score is often useful only for demonstrating that you have mastered APA style (90% correct is the usual standard for mastery). There are four versions of mastery tests for each unit, so you will have more than one opportunity to achieve mastery. Your instructor will tell you when you will be able to take a test and how scoring will be handled in your course.

There are several differences between taking mastery tests and taking familiarization or practice tests: You will not be allowed to keep the mastery tests, you will not be given an answer key to keep or the correct answers, and you will not be permitted to use the *Publication Manual* while you take the test. Your instructor will give you feedback by checking your answer sheet, marking any incorrect responses, and giving you your score. Your instructor may give you a blank answer key (which contains the APA codes for each question) with the questions you missed marked so you can find the correct answers in the *Publication Manual*.

The Publication Manual of the American Psychological Association

As has already been made clear, it is essential that you have a copy of the most recent edition of the *Publication Manual*. The *Publication Manual* is the official repository of information about APA format and style, and it comprises the standards for written materials in psychology as well in many other fields. *Mastering APA Style* is designed to teach about using, not to supplant, the *Publication Manual*. The module does not cover all of the rules, standards, and guidelines that are contained in the *Publication Manual*. It focuses on key elements of style and on teaching, by application, how to use the *Publication Manual* as a resource.

Other Style and Writing Guides

The *Publication Manual* is not exhaustive in its coverage of style guidelines. You need to be aware that there are other writing and style guides to consult on matters for which the *Publication Manual* does not provide guidance. Many institutions use the *Chicago Manual of Style* as their authority, as do the publishing departments of the American Psychological Association when the *Publication Manual* is insufficient. Some style guides are written for specific disciplines, such as *A Uniform System of Citation* for the legal profession and *Mathematics Into Type* for people who need to format complicated mathematical text. These kinds of style guides may be consulted when a special need arises.

The *Publication Manual* does devote two chapters to writing style. Again, although the information in these chapters presents fundamentals of good writing that apply to any kind of writing, the information is not exhaustive, and it focuses only on the more pertinent issues faced by writers of research articles. Should you discover that you need more assistance with writing, you should be aware that many good books on the topic exist. Chapter 9 of the *Publication Manual* lists some of these; you can also consult your reference librarian or an instructor in the English department at your school.

Model Manuscripts and Articles

One of the most effective ways to learn is through observing models. Your instructor may give you a set of examples of written work (published and unpublished, good and bad examples). An example of an unpublished manuscript should be particularly useful for you to see. Most of the time you will be asked to prepare manuscripts for course requirements, not publication. You may, of course, obtain samples of manuscripts that are written according to APA style from a library. APA publishes numerous scholarly journals and books, and any of these will be written in APA style. Be sure to obtain recent publications, however, to ensure that the current edition of the *Publication Manual* was followed.

Human Resources

Instructors and fellow students can be valuable resources. One of the most important skills a writer can have is that of being able to edit his or her own work. Rare is the person who produces a perfect first draft; the ability to revise and to correct errors comes with experience. You may lack this experience, and it is often difficult to be objective about your own work. *Mastering APA Style* is written in a way that fosters editorial skills. You are directed to give yourself feedback (by referring to the feedback version of exercises and to relevant sections of the *Publication Manual*) and to apply that feedback to new situations.

Instructors and fellow students can provide more opportunities for giving, receiving, and applying feedback. One potentially valuable experience is to exchange your work with another student and edit each other's work. By editing another student's paper, you can gain more real-world experience being an editor, you can probably be more objective about the flaws in a manuscript, and you can practice giving constructive criticism, all skills that will be useful to you when editing your own work.

Now You Are Ready to Begin

You have read chapter 1 and have defined your own reasons for learning APA style (each student will have different reasons), and you understand that this training module has been written to help you do so. You have read chapter 2, and you are reasonably familiar with the contents of the workbook and how to use it. You have your own copy of the *Publication Manual*. You have set your own goals or your instructor has set goals for you. If so, you are ready to use the workbook. If at any point you are unsure of what to do next or how to use any of the materials, review the pertinent sections of chapters 1 and 2. Of course, your instructor and your fellow students can be valuable resources.

Instructions for Taking the Term Paper Familiarization Test

Read each of the 40 numbered items and its corresponding set of possible responses, and choose the most accurate response. There is only one accurate response for each item. Some of the items instruct you to edit a segment of text, which you may do right on the test, and then to choose the response that characterizes what you have done (see the examples in "Instructions for Using the Workbook Materials"). Circle your choice on the test or mark your choice on the blank answer sheet provided for you at the end of the test. Take as much time as you need to complete the test, and consult the *Publication Manual* any time you wish. You may want to mark any item that gives you difficulty.

After you have responded to all of the test items, check your responses against the answer key at the end of the test. Make a notation next to any incorrect response on your answer sheet. Now, look at the APA codes that are listed next to each incorrect response or any response that you have flagged as being difficult. You may wonder why the answers are expressed in APA code intervals rather than a specific paragraph code. We found in field trials of the test materials that students attempted to learn the answer to a specific question rather than address a general weakness that they had in an area. When we gave them APA code intervals as feedback, students were less inclined to "figure out the tests" and more inclined to do what they were supposed to: master APA style. These codes refer you to the relevant sections of the *Publication Manual*. You can use this feedback to gauge how much work you need to do and in what areas and to decide what course of action to take next. You may want to review particular sections of the *Publication Manual* before attempting exercises. You may proceed to the exercises and complete them all, or you may choose to do only those that pertain to style issues with which you are unfamiliar. Keeping in mind that 90% is the criterion for mastery by the time you complete the workbook, your score on the familiarization test should be your guide. If you master the familiarization test with ease (scoring 90% correct or higher), you may even decide to do only the review exercises or go on to the practice test.

Sample "Edit the Following" Question

19. Edit the following for the punctuation of a series:

Theories of work motivation that emphasize the cognitive effects of information include a expectancy theory, b equity theory, and c goal-setting theory.

a. leave as is

b. Theories of work motivation that emphasize the cognitive effects of information include (a) expectancy theory, (b) equity theory, and (c) goal-setting theory.

c. Theories of work motivation that emphasize the cognitive effects of information include a) expectancy theory, b) equity theory, and c) goal-setting theory.

d. Theories of work motivation that emphasize the cognitive effects of information include: a. expectancy theory, b. equity theory, and c. goal-setting theory.

Instructions for Completing the Exercises

As you can see in the sample learning exercise below, each exercise consists of three elements: the text of the exercise, the APA code, and an index number. The APA code cites the section of the *Publication Manual* that the exercise addresses. The index number is an inventory number; you should ignore it. Approach the exercises as follows: Do not look at the feedback version on the left-hand page until you complete working with the draft version on the right-hand page. Read the text in the draft version (right-hand page). Examine the text that is shaded and decide whether it is correct as is or needs to be edited. Write changes on or above the text lines. If you wish to consult the *Publication Manual,* refer to the APA codes to find the pertinent sections. You may complete all of the exercises and then look at the feedback version, or you may look at the feedback version after completing each exercise.

Read the feedback version of each exercise (left-hand page) and examine the text that is shaded. Compare your editing with the correct version. If your response does not agree with the feedback version, you may want to review relevant sections of the *Publication Manual.*

Sample Learning Exercise

Draft

The training technique which was easiest to administer turned out to be the one that was most effective.

APA CODE: 2.10   INDEX NUMBER: 02

Feedback

The training technique that was easiest to administer turned out to be the one that was most effective.

APA CODE: 2.10   INDEX NUMBER: 02

For integrative exercises (see the example below), read the text of the draft version and edit as needed by writing changes on or above the text lines. None of the text is shaded; you must decide which style points are being addressed. Consult the *Publication Manual* by referring to the APA codes listed with the exercise. When you have finished editing the draft version, consult the feedback version. With integrative exercises, it is probably best if you do this after each exercise, while your reasoning is still fresh in your mind. Essential changes will be shaded on the feedback version, or the exercise will indicate that the text is "correct as is."

Sample Integrative Exercise

Draft: Headings and Series and General Typing Instructions

Irrational fear

Fear of Living Organisms

AMPHIBIAN PHOBIAS

Fear of salamanders

Forest newt phobia. There is a salamander found near Salamanca, New York, a tiny pink and white forest newt, that has been shown to arouse tremendous fear in people who already have (a) a spaghetti phobia, (b) a worm phobia, and (c) mysophobia.

APA CODES: 3.30–3.33, 5.10, 5.12   INDEX NUMBER: 01

Feedback: Headings and Series and General Typing Instructions

IRRATIONAL FEAR

Fear of Living Organisms

Amphibian Phobias

Fear of Salamanders

Forest newt phobia. There is a salamander found near Salamanca, New York, a tiny pink and white forest newt, that has been shown to arouse tremendous fear in people who already have (a) a spaghetti phobia, (b) a worm phobia, and (c) mysophobia.

APA CODES: 3.30–3.33, 5.10, 5.12   INDEX NUMBER: 01

CHAPTER 3

Term Paper Unit

3

The purpose of this unit is to familiarize you with the basic principles of APA style, such as grammar, spelling and hyphenation, and so forth, as they apply to writing term papers, essays, and literature reviews. This unit is divided into four components: the familiarization test, learning exercises and integrative exercises, the practice test, and review exercises. Begin by taking the familiarization test, which will help you to identify what you do and do not know about APA style.

Term Paper Familiarization Test

By taking this 40-question multiple-choice test, you will be able to determine the style principles with which you need more practice. There are two answer sheets at the end of the test, one with blanks for you to write in your answers and the other containing the correct answers.

Beside each blank you will find the APA code (e.g., 1.3, 2.13) that indicates where you can find the answer to that question in the *Publication Manual*. These APA codes correspond to the numbered sections of the *Publication Manual*. Read each test item and the possible responses, and write the letter of the response on the blank answer sheet. You may consult the *Publication Manual* at any time. It may be useful to mark questions you found to be difficult.

After taking this test, check your answers against the answer key and score your test, but count only those questions that you answered without using the *Publication Manual*. If the total number of incorrect answers plus looked-up answers is 8 or more (20% or more incorrect), we advise you to complete all of the exercises that follow this test. If you did well on the test (i.e., 36 of 40 correct), you may want to skip the learning exercises and take the practice test that follows the exercises in this term paper unit or take a mastery test.

TERM PAPER FAMILIARIZATION TEST

1. In contrast to empirical or theoretical articles, review articles

    a. define and clarify a problem.
    b. summarize previous investigations.
    c. identify relations, contradictions, or inconsistencies in the literature.
    d. suggest steps for future research.
    e. do all of the above.

2. When listing an author of a paper, it is incorrect to

    a. give titles (PhD or OFM).
    b. spell out the middle name.
    c. use informal names (Ronnie Reagan).
    d. do all of the above.

3. In casual conversation the word *since* is synonymous with _____, but in scientific writing it should be used only in its temporal meaning.

    a. *however*
    b. *because*
    c. *after*
    d. all of the above

4. Good economy of expression may be achieved through using

    a. short words.
    b. short sentences.
    c. simple declarative sentences.
    d. short paragraphs.
    e. all of the above.

5. The phrase "the experiment demonstrated" is an example of which of the following writing errors?

    a. ambiguity
    b. redundancy
    c. attributing a human characteristic to a nonhuman source
    d. none of the above

6. Which of the following sentences contains the preferable use of verb tense and voice?

    a. The same results have been shown by Ramirez (1980).

    b. Ramirez (1980) shows the same results.

    c. Ramirez (1980) showed the same results.

    d. Ramirez (1980) had shown the same results.

7. Which of the following sentences is an example of correct agreement between the pronoun and its antecedent?

    a. The rats that completed the task successfully were rewarded.

    b. Neither the highest scorer nor the lowest scorer had any doubt about their

        competence.

    c. The group improved their scores 30%.

    d. All of the above are correct.
    e. None of the above is correct.

8. Edit the following for the placement of the modifier *only*:

   Although the authors reported the data for the mild and extreme patients in the placebo condition, they only reported the data for the extreme patients in the treatment condition.

   a. leave as is

   b. Although the authors reported the data for the mild and extreme patients in the placebo condition, they reported only the data for the extreme patients in the treatment condition.

   c. Although the authors reported the data for the mild and extreme patients in the placebo condition, they reported the data for only the extreme patients in the treatment condition.

   d. Although the authors reported the data for the mild and extreme patients in the placebo condition, they reported the data for the extreme patients only in the treatment condition.

9. Edit the following for the use of subordinate conjunctions:

   Since left-handers constitute a minority of the population, there are less likely to be appropriate models for them to watch.

   a. leave as is

   b. Because left-handers constitute a minority of the population, there are less likely to be appropriate models for them to watch.

   c. Although left-handers constitute a minority of the population, there are less likely to be appropriate models for them to watch.

   d. While left-handers constitute a minority of the population, there are less likely to be appropriate models for them to watch.

10. Edit the following for sentence structure:

   Erikson's psychosocial theory emphasizes not only developmental stages but also the role of the ego.

   a. leave as is

   b. Erikson's psychosocial theory not only emphasizes developmental stages but also the role of the ego.

   c. Erikson's psychosocial theory emphasizes not only developmental stages but also the role of the ego, as well.

   d. Erikson's psychosocial theory emphasizes not only developmental stages but neither the role of the ego.

11. Edit the following for the use of nonsexist language:

It has been suggested that the major factor giving man a performance advantage over other primates on many cognitive tasks is that the tasks have been selected and administered by other men.

a. leave as is

b. It has been suggested that the major factor giving the species of man a performance advantage over other primates on many cognitive tasks is that the tasks have been selected and administered by men of the same species.

c. It has been suggested that the major factor giving human beings a performance advantage over other primates on many cognitive tasks is that the tasks have been selected and administered by other human beings.

d. It has been suggested that the major factor giving human beings (men or women) a performance advantage over other primates on many cognitive tasks is that the tasks have been selected and administered by other human beings.

12. Edit the following for avoiding ethnic bias:

Because of their cultural deprivation, children in Third World countries have fewer opportunities to develop our moral values.

a. leave as is

b. Because of cultural differences, children in Third World countries may develop moral values different from those of children in Western countries.

c. Because of their cultural deprivation, children in Third World countries may not develop higher moral values.

d. Because of their cultural experiences, children in Third World countries have fewer opportunities to develop our moral values.

13. Edit the following for punctuation:

The James-Lange theory of emotion states that our emotional experience is caused by our awareness of our bodily reaction to some stimulus: Schachter and Singer (1962) proposed that a cognitive evaluation mediates between the bodily reaction and the subjective emotion.

a. leave as is

b. The James-Lange theory of emotion states that our emotional experience is caused by our awareness of our bodily reaction to some stimulus. Schachter and Singer (1962) proposed that a cognitive evaluation mediates between the bodily reaction and the subjective emotion.

c. The James-Lange theory of emotion states that our emotional experience is caused by our awareness of our bodily reaction to some stimulus--Schachter and Singer (1962) proposed that a cognitive evaluation mediates between the bodily reaction and the subjective emotion.

d. The James-Lange theory of emotion states that our emotional experience is caused by our awareness of our bodily reaction to some stimulus. And Schachter and Singer (1962) proposed that a cognitive evaluation mediates between the bodily reaction and the subjective emotion.

14. Which of the following phrases is correctly punctuated?

a. the study, by Jones Davis and Stewart (1972)

b. the study by Jones, Davis, and Stewart (1972)

c. the study by Jones, Davis, and Stewart, (1972)

d. the study by Jones, Davis and Stewart (1972)

e. the study by Jones Davis and Stewart (1972)

15. Edit the following for the punctuation of a reference entry:

Strunk, W., Jr., & White, E. B. (1979). *The elements of style* (3rd ed.). New York. Macmillan.

a. leave as is

b. Strunk, W., Jr., & White, E. B. (1979). *The elements of style* (3rd ed.). New York: Macmillan.

c. Strunk, W., Jr., & White, E. B. (1979). *The elements of style* (3rd ed.). New York, Macmillan.

d. Strunk, W., Jr., & White, E. B. (1979). *The elements of style* (3rd ed.). New York/Macmillan.

16. When is the dash used?
    a. to extend a thought
    b. instead of commas to set off restrictive clauses
    c. never in APA articles
    d. to indicate a sudden interruption in the continuity of a sentence

17. Edit the following for the correct way to report verbatim instructions:

    The participants were instructed to COMPLETE EACH SENTENCE BASED ON YOUR OWN FEELINGS AT THIS MOMENT.

    a. leave as is
    b. The participants were instructed to *complete each sentence based on your own feelings at this moment.*
    c. The participants were instructed to "complete each sentence based on your own feelings at this moment."
    d. The participants were instructed to 'complete each sentence based on your own feelings at this moment.'

18. When quoting long sections of material (e.g., verbatim instructions to participants of more than 40 words),
    a. set the quote off with double quotation marks.
    b. indent and use a block format without any quotation marks.
    c. use a single quotation at the beginning and the end of the quotation.
    d. use double quotation marks and single-spacing.

19. Edit the following for the punctuation of a series:

    Theories of work motivation that emphasize the cognitive effects of information include *a* expectancy theory, *b* equity theory, and *c* goal-setting theory.

    a. leave as is
    b. Theories of work motivation that emphasize the cognitive effects of information include (a) expectancy theory, (b) equity theory, and (c) goal-setting theory.
    c. Theories of work motivation that emphasize the cognitive effects of information include a) expectancy theory, b) equity theory, and c) goal-setting theory.
    d. Theories of work motivation that emphasize the cognitive effects of information include: a. expectancy theory, b. equity theory, and c. goal-setting theory.

20. Which of the following examples should not be hyphenated?
    a. role-playing technique
    b. super-ordinate variable
    c. six-trial problem
    d. high-anxiety group
    e. all of the above

21. In titles of books and articles, initial letters are capitalized in

    a. major words when titles appear in regular text.
    b. words of four letters or more when titles appear in regular text.
    c. the second word in a hyphenated compound when titles appear in regular text.
    d. major words and words of four letters or more when titles appear in reference lists.
    e. all of the above except d.

22. From the following choices, select the sentence with the correct use of italics:

    a. She published her results in the *Journal of Interpersonal Relations and Social Behavior*.

    b. She published *her* results in the Journal of Interpersonal Relations and Social Behavior.

    c. When the *participants* read the nonsense syllable gux, they had to soothe their fearful partners.

    d. *Albino rabbits*, oryctolagus cuniculus, were given unconditional positive regard in both experimental groups.

23. Edit the following for use of abbreviations:

    According to Pavlov (1927), the conditioned stimulus (CS) should be delivered about 1 s before the unconditioned stimulus (US).

    a. leave as is

    b. According to Pavlov (1927), the conditioned stimulus (CS) should be delivered about 1 second before the unconditioned stimulus (US).

    c. According to Pavlov (1927), the conditioned stimulus (CS) should be delivered about 1 sec. before the unconditioned stimulus (US).

    d. According to Pavlov (1927), the CS should be delivered about 1 s before the US.

24. The headings of a manuscript

    a. reveal the logical organization of the paper to the reader.
    b. should be at the same level for topics of equal importance.
    c. need not be numbered.
    d. All of the above are correct.

25. Which example is correct for an article in which four levels of heading are required?

a.

A History of Psychology

Early Laboratories

Harvard Laboratories

    James's basement.

b.

A HISTORY OF PSYCHOLOGY

Early Laboratories

Harvard Laboratories

    James's Basement.

c.

A HISTORY OF PSYCHOLOGY

Early Laboratories

Harvard Laboratories

    James's basement.

d.

A HISTORY OF PSYCHOLOGY

Early Laboratories

Harvard Laboratories

James's Basement

26. Identify the error in the following quotation:

The author speculated that "negative exemplars within the self-concept are more confidently known than affirmative exemplars" (Brinthaup, 1983).

a. The quote is correctly cited.
b. The quote should be in block form.
c. Quotation marks are not necessary.
d. A page number should be cited.

27. Edit the following for the citation of a reference in text:

Gazzaniga, 1967, flashed pictures to the right or left visual field of each patient whose corpus callosum had been surgically severed.

a. leave as is

b. Gazzaniga/1967 flashed pictures to the right or left visual field of each patient whose corpus callosum had been surgically severed.

c. Gazzaniga (Gazzaniga, 1967) flashed pictures to the right or left visual field of each patient whose corpus callosum had been surgically severed.

d. Gazzaniga (1967) flashed pictures to the right or left visual field of each patient whose corpus callosum had been surgically severed.

28. Edit the following for the citation of a reference in text:

In one of the earliest studies (Anand, Chhina, & Singh, 1961), researchers presented a variety of stimuli to a yogi as he meditated. Anand, Chhina, and Singh reported no disruption of the yogi's alpha wave--as indicated by EEG recordings--by a tuning fork or a hand clap.

a. leave as is

b. In one of the earliest studies (Anand, Chhina, & Singh, 1961), researchers presented a variety of stimuli to a yogi as he meditated. Anand, Chhina, et al. reported no disruption of the yogi's alpha wave--as indicated by EEG recordings --by a tuning fork or a hand clap.

c. In one of the earliest studies (Anand, Chhina, & Singh, 1961), researchers presented a variety of stimuli to a yogi as he meditated. Anand et al. reported no disruption of the yogi's alpha wave--as indicated by EEG recordings--by a tuning fork or a hand clap.

d. In one of the earliest studies (Anand, Chhina, & Singh, 1961), researchers presented a variety of stimuli to a yogi as he meditated. Anand et al. reported no disruption of the yogi's alpha wave--as indicated by EEG recordings--by a tuning fork or a hand clap.

29. When a publication has no author,
   a. the text citation must have the entire title of the publication.
   b. the text citation should use the publisher's name.
   c. no citation is necessary.
   d. none of the above is true.

30. Edit the following for the citation of references in text:

> Personality changes may also occur later in life (Neugarten, 1973; Neugarten & Hagestad, 1976; Neugarten, 1977).

a. leave as is

b. Personality changes may also occur later in life (Neugarten, 1973, 1977; Neugarten & Hagestad, 1976).

c. Personality changes may also occur later in life (Neugarten, 1973, 1977; & Hagestad, 1976).

d. Personality changes may also occur later in life (Neugarten, 1973, Neugarten & Hagestad, 1976; ibid., 1977).

31. When citing a specific part of a source, be sure to give
    a. the authors' names.
    b. the year of publication.
    c. a page number if a quotation is cited.
    d. all of the above.

32. Who has the responsibility to ensure that references are accurate and complete?
    a. an editor
    b. a proofreader
    c. a printer
    d. an author

33. Edit the following for ordering the references in a reference list. Choose the sequence of numbers that indicates the correct order of the four references. (*Note:* The numbers are not part of APA style but are used here for brevity.)

> 1. Lazarus, R. S. (1969). *Psychological stress and the coping process.* New York: McGraw-Hill.
>
> 2. Lazarus, A. A. (1977). Has behavior therapy outlived its usefulness? *American Psychologist, 32,* 550-554.
>
> 3. Smith, M. L., & Glass, G. V. (1977). Meta-analysis of psychotherapy outcome studies. *American Psychologist, 32,* 752-760.
>
> 4. Smith, D. (1982). Trends in counseling and psychotherapy. *American Psychologist, 37,* 802-809.

a. leave as is (i.e., 1, 2, 3, 4)
b. 2, 1, 4, 3
c. 2, 3, 1, 4
d. 4, 3, 2, 1

34. Edit the following for the application of APA reference style:

   Olds, J., & Milner, P. Positive reinforcement produced by electrical stimulation of septal areas and other regions of rat brains. *Journal of Comparative and Physiological Psychology*, (1954), 47, 419-427.

   a. leave as is

   b. Olds, J., & Milner, P. Positive reinforcement produced by electrical stimulation of septal areas and other regions of rat brains. *Journal of Comparative and Physiological Psychology*, 1954, 47, 419-427.

   c. Olds, J., & Milner, P. 1954. Positive reinforcement produced by electrical stimulation of septal areas and other regions of rat brains. *Journal of Comparative and Physiological Psychology*, 47, 419-427.

   d. Olds, J., & Milner, P. (1954). Positive reinforcement produced by electrical stimulation of septal areas and other regions of rat brains. *Journal of Comparative and Physiological Psychology*, 47, 419-427.

35. Edit the following for the application of APA reference style:

   Hilgard, E. R., & Bower, G. H. (1975). *Theories of learning, fourth ed.* Englewood Cliffs, NJ: Prentice Hall.

   a. leave as is

   b. Hilgard, E. R., & Bower, G. H. (1975). *Theories of learning, 4th ed.* Englewood Cliffs, NJ: Prentice Hall.

   c. Hilgard, E. R., & Bower, G. H. (1975). *Theories of learning* (4th ed.). Englewood Cliffs, NJ: Prentice Hall.

   d. Hilgard, E. R., & Bower, G. H. (1975, 4th ed.). *Theories of learning.* Englewood Cliffs, NJ: Prentice Hall.

36. When typing a paper,
   a. double-space after headings and between paragraphs and reference list citations; single-space elsewhere.
   b. double-space throughout the paper.
   c. single-space between the lines of table headings.
   d. double-space everything except triple-space after major headings.

37. Edit the following by selecting the correct spacing and margin arrangement for the first sentence of a paragraph:

> The mating and social behaviors of many species change dramatically when they are removed from their natural environments, whether to be domesticated or to be exhibited in zoos.

a. leave as is

b.   The mating and social behaviors of many species change dramatically when they are removed from their natural environments, whether to be domesticated or to be exhibited in zoos.

c.   The mating and social behaviors of many species change dramatically when they are removed from their natural environments, whether to be domesticated or to be exhibited in zoos.

d. The mating and social behaviors of many species change dramatically when they are removed from their natural environments, whether to be domesticated or to be exhibited in zoos.

38. Corrections should be

a. written in the margins of the manuscript.
b. made by covering the error with correction tape, paper, or fluid and then typing the correction on top.
c. typed on separate half pages and attached to the pages to be corrected.
d. made in the word-processing file and printed out.
e. b and d.

39. One space should follow

a. semicolons.
b. colons in two-part titles.
c. periods in the initials of personal names.
d. all of the above.
e. none of the above.

40. Edit the following for the presentation of a series:

The researchers attempted to determine the relation between the age of the mother at the child's birth and (1) the child's intellectual development, (2) the child's social development, and (3) the mother's personal adjustment.

a. leave as is

b. The researchers attempted to determine the relation between the age of the mother at the child's birth and (a) the child's intellectual development, (b) the child's social development, and (c) the mother's personal adjustment.

c. The researchers attempted to determine the relation between the age of the mother at the child's birth and (*a*) the child's intellectual development, (*b*) the child's social development, and (c) the mother's personal adjustment.

d. The researchers attempted to determine the relation between the age of the mother at the child's birth and (A) the child's intellectual development, (B) the child's social development, and (C) the mother's personal adjustment.

TERM PAPER FAMILIARIZATION TEST
ANSWER SHEET AND FEEDBACK REPORT

Student Name _____ **Date** _____

Question Number	Answer	APA Codes	Question Number	Answer	APA Codes
1	_____	1.03–1.05	21	_____	3.12–3.18
2	_____	1.06–1.08	22	_____	3.19
3	_____	2.01–2.02	23	_____	3.20–3.29
4	_____	2.03–2.05	24	_____	3.30–3.33
5	_____	2.03–2.05	25	_____	3.30–3.33
6	_____	2.06–2.07	26	_____	3.34–3.41
7	_____	2.08–2.11	27	_____	3.94–3.103
8	_____	2.08–2.11	28	_____	3.94–3.103
9	_____	2.08–2.11	29	_____	3.94–3.103
10	_____	2.08–2.11	30	_____	3.94–3.103
11	_____	2.13–2.17	31	_____	3.94–3.103
12	_____	2.13–2.17	32	_____	4.01–4.04
13	_____	3.01–3.09	33	_____	4.01–4.04
14	_____	3.01–3.09	34	_____	4.01–4.04
15	_____	3.01–3.09	35	_____	4.01–4.04
16	_____	3.01–3.09	36	_____	5.01–5.08
17	_____	3.01–3.09	37	_____	5.01–5.08
18	_____	3.01–3.09	38	_____	5.01–5.08
19	_____	3.01–3.09	39	_____	5.09–5.13
20	_____	3.10–3.11	40	_____	5.09–5.13

NUMBER CORRECT _____

TERM PAPER FAMILIARIZATION TEST
ANSWER KEY

Question Number	Answer	APA Codes	Question Number	Answer	APA Codes
1	e	1.03–1.05	21	e	3.12–3.18
2	d	1.06–1.08	22	a	3.19
3	b	2.01–2.02	23	a	3.20–3.29
4	e	2.03–2.05	24	d	3.30–3.33
5	c	2.03–2.05	25	a	3.30–3.33
6	c	2.06–2.07	26	d	3.34–3.41
7	a	2.08–2.11	27	d	3.94–3.103
8	c	2.08–2.11	28	d	3.94–3.103
9	b	2.08–2.11	29	d	3.94–3.103
10	a	2.08–2.11	30	b	3.94–3.103
11	c	2.13–2.17	31	d	3.94–3.103
12	b	2.13–2.17	32	d	4.01–4.04
13	b	3.01–3.09	33	b	4.01–4.04
14	b	3.01–3.09	34	d	4.01–4.04
15	b	3.01–3.09	35	c	4.01–4.04
16	d	3.01–3.09	36	b	5.01–5.08
17	c	3.01–3.09	37	b	5.01–5.08
18	b	3.01–3.09	38	e	5.01–5.08
19	b	3.01–3.09	39	d	5.09–5.13
20	b	3.10–3.11	40	b	5.09–5.13

Term Paper Learning Exercises and Integrative Exercises

The learning exercises and integrative exercises appear in two versions: *draft*, which may or may not contain errors, and *feedback*, which shows the corrections. The feedback (correct) version always appears on the left-hand page and the draft (incorrect) version on the right. There are APA codes under each section title that indicate where the specific style rules can be found in the *Publication Manual;* APA codes corresponding to the sections of the *Publication Manual* are also below each exercise.

There are two types of exercises: learning (short) exercises and integrative exercises. Learning exercises are brief excerpts of text that address one or two components of APA style (e.g., commas, capitalization). The component that is being targeted (i.e., in need of correction) is shaded. Looking at the draft version on the right-hand page, read the text and decide whether the shaded text is correct or incorrect. Write corrections on the workbook page directly above the errors. Consult the *Publication Manual* at any time. Check your answers against the feedback version of the same exercise on the left to see whether you edited the exercise correctly. The feedback version will state "correct as is," or the correctly edited material will be shaded. You may complete the exercises and check the corrections one by one or section by section.

Integrative exercises consist of a paragraph or page of text that you need to edit. The components in need of correction are not shaded, but the errors in each integrative exercise are all related to the style rules applied in the preceding learning exercises. For example, if you are working in the section on italics, the errors you will be looking for involve the use of italics. Read the text carefully and edit it as you deem appropriate, marking corrections directly on the draft version. The corrections are shaded on the feedback (left-hand) page. Integrative exercises follow the learning exercises. After completing the exercises, you can take the term paper practice test that follows the exercises, or you can ask your instructor to give you a mastery test.

Parts of a Manuscript and Typing the Parts of a Manuscript
APA Codes: 1.06–1.14, 5.15–5.17

NOTES:

Effects of Long-Term Memory on Artificial Intelligence

Ebbin G. Haus

Mnemonia University

APA CODE: 1.06   INDEX NUMBER: 01

Can I Give You a Hand, a Hand, ... a Hand? Hyperaltruism in

the Octopus

Minnie Foote and Hans Goode

Submarine Social Center, Atlantis University

APA CODE: 1.06   INDEX NUMBER: 02

Running head: BOVINE BARNYARD BANTER

Naturalistic Observation of Barnyard Banter:

Pig-Latin Epithets Overheard During Bovine Horseplay

Hans Clever and Du Li Tal

Interspecies Babble Institute, Babylonia, Babylon

APA CODE: 5.15   INDEX NUMBER: 01

Parts of a Manuscript and Typing the Parts of a Manuscript
APA Codes: 1.06–1.15, 5.15–5.17

These exercises cover typing the title page, author affiliation, and running heads (see the *Publication Manual*, sections 1.06–1.15 and 5.15–5.17). Mark corrections directly on the right-hand page and compare your responses with the correct answers on the left-hand page. When you are finished with this section, go on to the next section in which you need practice.

A Study of the Effects of LTM on AI

Ebbin G. Haus

Mnemonia University

APA CODE: 1.06   INDEX NUMBER: 01

Can I Give You a Hand, a Hand, … a Hand? Hyperaltruism in

the Octopus

Foote, Minnie   Goode, Hans

Submarine Social Center, Atlantis University

APA CODE: 1.06   INDEX NUMBER: 02

Running head: BOVINE BARNYARD BANTER

Naturalistic Observation of Barnyard Banter:
Pig-Latin Epithets Overheard During Bovine Horseplay

Hans Clever and Du Li Tal
Interspecies Babble Institute, Babylon, Babylonia

APA CODE: 5.15   INDEX NUMBER: 01

Latent Hostility in Tongue-in-Cheek Expressions: Phylogenetic
Comparison of Rattlesnakes (*Crotolus bitus*) and Humans (*Homo sapiens*)

Rip Tyle

Desert Rock State College

V. Shus and Hugh Moor

School of Hard Knocks College

Correct as is.

APA CODE: 5.15   INDEX NUMBER: 02

Meta-Analysis of Predictive Validity of the Personal Interview for
Selecting Apiary Workers: A Stinging Critique

Queen Bea H. Ivy

Wasp Personnel Consultants, Buzztown, New Colony

APA CODE: 5.15   INDEX NUMBER: 03

Cool as a Cucumber: Psychophysiological Responses of a Vegetative
Organism to Social and Emotional Stressors

Bess T. Green, Vera Thigsken, and Sal Ad O'yil

Seedy Character College

APA CODE: 5.15   INDEX NUMBER: 04

Running head: COMPARATIVE HOSTILITY IN RATTLESNAKES

Latent Hostility in Tongue-in-Cheek Expressions: Phylogenetic Comparison

of Rattlesnakes (*Crotolus bitus*) and Humans (*Homo sapiens*)

Rip Tyle

Desert Rock State College

V. Shus and Hugh Moor

School of Hard Knocks College

APA CODE: 5.15   INDEX NUMBER: 02

Running head: VALIDITY OF DRONE INTERVIEWS

Meta-Analysis of Predictive Validity of the Personal Interview for

Selecting Apiary Workers: A Stinging Critique

Queen Bea H. Ivy

Wasp Personnel Consultants, Buzztown, New Colony

APA CODE: 5.15   INDEX NUMBER: 03

Running head: PSYCHOPHYSIOLOGY OF STRESSED CUCUMBERS

COOL AS A CUCUMBER: PSYCHOPHYSIOLOGICAL RESPONSES OF A VEGETATIVE

ORGANISM TO SOCIAL AND EMOTIONAL STRESSORS

Bess T. Green, Vera Thigsken, and Sal Ad O'yil

Seedy Character College

APA CODE: 5.15   INDEX NUMBER: 04

Effects of Fowl-Language Deprivation on Comprehension

of Irony and Metaphor by Toms and Chicks

Po Li Tri and S. R. Khazzam

Egghead University

APA CODE: 5.15   INDEX NUMBER: 05

Vicious Circle

3

Vicious Circle Behavior and Parental Child Abuse

APA CODE: 5.17   INDEX NUMBER: 01

Integrative Exercise: Parts of a Manuscript and Typing the Parts of a Manuscript

Effects of Severe

1

Running head: SEVERE WEATHER AND OLFACTION

Effects of Severe Weather Conditions on Olfactory Sensitivity

O. Dora Testor, Cy Clone, Harry Cane, and Thor Naddo

University of the North

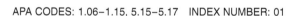

APA CODES: 1.06–1.15, 5.15–5.17   INDEX NUMBER: 01

Effects of Fowl-Language Deprivation on Comprehension

of Irony and Metaphor by Toms and Chicks

by Tri, Po Li and Khazzam, S. R.

Department of Psychology

Egghead University

APA CODE: 5.15   INDEX NUMBER: 05

Vicious Circle

3

Vicious Circle Behavior and Parental Child Abuse

APA CODE: 5.17   INDEX NUMBER: 01

Integrative Exercise: Parts of a Manuscript and Typing the Parts of a Manuscript

1

A STUDY OF EFFECTS OF SEVERE WEATHER CONDITIONS ON OLFACTORY

SENSITIVITY

O. Dora Testor   Cy Clone, Harry Cane and Thor Naddo

Department of Psychology   Department of Psychometeorology

University of the North

Running head: SEVERE WEATHER AND OLFACTION

APA CODES: 1.06–1.15, 5.15–5.17   INDEX NUMBER: 01

Grammar
APA Codes: 2.06–2.12

NOTES:

Practitioners have experienced the dilemma for years.

APA CODE: 2.06   INDEX NUMBER: 01

The experimenter then asked the child to name the object.

APA CODE: 2.06   INDEX NUMBER: 02

Results

The social facilitation effect in Experiment 2 replicated our findings in Experiment 1.

APA CODE: 2.06   INDEX NUMBER: 03

Schachter and Singer (1962) proposed that emotional states have physiological and cognitive components.

Correct as is.   APA CODE: 2.06   INDEX NUMBER: 04

Cognitive psychologists have used the computer metaphor since the 1960s.

APA CODE: 2.06   INDEX NUMBER: 05

The leader as well as the group members was asked to perform the second task individually.

APA CODE: 2.07   INDEX NUMBER: 01

The criterion for learning was 10 consecutive correct choices.

APA CODE: 2.07   INDEX NUMBER: 02

As with most illusory phenomena, this illusion provides an interesting demonstration but generates few experiments.

APA CODE: 2.07   INDEX NUMBER:

Grammar
APA Codes: 2.06–2.12

In this group of exercises you can practice and learn about verb tense, subject–verb agreement, pronouns, misplaced and dangling modifiers, relative pronouns and subordinate conjunctions, and parallel construction (see the *Publication Manual*, sections 2.06–2.12). Mark corrections directly on the right-hand page, and compare your responses with the correct answers on the left-hand page. When you are finished with this section, go on to the next section in which you need practice.

The dilemma has been experienced by practitioners for years.

APA CODE: 2.06   INDEX NUMBER: 01

The experimenter then asks the child to name the object.

APA CODE: 2.06   INDEX NUMBER: 02

Results

The social facilitation effect in Experiment 2 replicates our findings in Experiment 1.

APA CODE: 2.06   INDEX NUMBER: 03

Schachter and Singer (1962) proposed that emotional states have physiological and cognitive components.

APA CODE: 2.06   INDEX NUMBER: 04

Cognitive psychologists used the computer metaphor since the 1960s.

APA CODE: 2.06   INDEX NUMBER: 05

The leader as well as the group members were asked to perform the second task individually.

APA CODE: 2.07   INDEX NUMBER: 01

The criteria for learning was 10 consecutive correct choices.

APA CODE: 2.07   INDEX NUMBER: 02

As with most illusory phenomenon, this illusion provides an interesting demonstration but generates few experiments.

APA CODE: 2.07   INDEX NUMBER:

The data confirm█ the inhibitory hypothesis.

APA CODE: 2.07   INDEX NUMBER: 04

The moving stimuli `were` the most effective.

APA CODE: 2.07   INDEX NUMBER: 05

The group of experts `was` to arrive at one solution.

`Correct as is.`   APA CODE: 2.07   INDEX NUMBER: 06

The group of experts `were` tested individually to attain ideal scores to present as targets.

APA CODE: 2.07   INDEX NUMBER: 07

The set of programs `was` selected to include a wide range of role models.

`Correct as is.`   APA CODE: 2.07   INDEX NUMBER: 08

The faculty `were` paired with the students to form 20 expert-novice teams.

APA CODE: 2.07   INDEX NUMBER: 09

None of the flavors `were` familiar to the rat.

`Correct as is.`   APA CODE: 2.07   INDEX NUMBER: 10

Neither the child nor the parents `were` able to see the observer.

APA CODE: 2.07   INDEX NUMBER: 11

After each respondent made a preliminary rating based on the picture, `he or she` read the detailed information and made a second rating.

APA CODE: 2.08   INDEX NUMBER: 01

The clients `who` achieved a score above the criterion were allowed to participate in the group activity for that day.

APA CODE: 2.08   INDEX NUMBER: 02

The data confirms the inhibitory hypothesis.

APA CODE: 2.07   INDEX NUMBER: 04

The moving stimuli was the most effective.

APA CODE: 2.07   INDEX NUMBER: 05

The group of experts was to arrive at one solution.

APA CODE: 2.07   INDEX NUMBER: 06

The group of experts was tested individually to attain ideal scores to present as targets.

APA CODE: 2.07   INDEX NUMBER: 07

The set of programs was selected to include a wide range of role models.

APA CODE: 2.07   INDEX NUMBER: 08

The faculty was paired with the students to form 20 expert-novice teams.

APA CODE: 2.07   INDEX NUMBER: 09

None of the flavors were familiar to the rat.

APA CODE: 2.07   INDEX NUMBER: 10

Neither the child nor the parents was able to see the observer.

APA CODE: 2.07   INDEX NUMBER: 11

After each respondent made a preliminary rating based on the picture, they read the detailed information and made a second rating.

APA CODE: 2.08   INDEX NUMBER: 01

The clients that achieved a score above the criterion were allowed to participate in the group activity for that day.

APA CODE: 2.08   INDEX NUMBER: 02

The monkeys that showed right-paw dominance were trained to select with their left paws.

APA CODE: 2.08   INDEX NUMBER: 03

A second group of respondents rated, on attractiveness, the person whom the members of the first group selected most frequently as a partner.

APA CODE: 2.08   INDEX NUMBER: 04

Using the narrative technique, the raters evaluated the therapists.

APA CODE: 2.09   INDEX NUMBER: 01

In the overt condition, the children made a total of only 12 incorrect classifications.

APA CODE: 2.09   INDEX NUMBER: 02

The parent recorded each utterance the child made. After counting the number of utterances, the parent gave the child the appropriate story to read.

APA CODE: 2.09   INDEX NUMBER: 03

The format that was easiest to decipher during pilot testing was used during the main part of the experiment.

Correct as is.   APA CODE: 2.10   INDEX NUMBER: 01

The training technique that was easiest to administer turned out to be the one that was most effective.

APA CODE: 2.10   INDEX NUMBER: 02

Error trials, which were equally frequent in the two conditions, were eliminated from the analysis.

APA CODE: 2.10   INDEX NUMBER: 03

Although the group that was returned to the original context made more correct identifications, they also made more false alarms.

APA CODE: 2.10   INDEX NUMBER: 04

The monkeys who showed right-paw dominance were trained to select with their left paws.

APA CODE: 2.08   INDEX NUMBER: 03

A second group of respondents rated, on attractiveness, the person who the members of the first group selected most frequently as a partner.

APA CODE: 2.08   INDEX NUMBER: 04

The raters evaluated the therapists using the narrative technique.

APA CODE: 2.09   INDEX NUMBER: 01

In the overt condition, the children only made a total of 12 incorrect classifications.

APA CODE: 2.09   INDEX NUMBER: 02

The parent recorded each utterance the child made. After counting the number of utterances, the child was given the appropriate story to read.

APA CODE: 2.09   INDEX NUMBER: 03

The format that was easiest to decipher during pilot testing was used during the main part of the experiment.

APA CODE: 2.10   INDEX NUMBER: 01

The training technique which was easiest to administer turned out to be the one that was most effective.

APA CODE: 2.10   INDEX NUMBER: 02

Error trials, that were equally frequent in the two conditions, were eliminated from the analysis.

APA CODE: 2.10   INDEX NUMBER: 03

While the group that was returned to the original context made more correct identifications, they also made more false alarms.

APA CODE: 2.10   INDEX NUMBER: 04

Behavioral treatments were judged easier to administer by the therapists, whereas client-centered methods were judged more enjoyable by the clients.

APA CODE: 2.10   INDEX NUMBER: 05

Because there were no significant main effects or interactions involving experimenter, the data from the different experimenters were pooled.

APA CODE: 2.10   INDEX NUMBER: 06

Since the last edition of this text, there has been a major revision in the research paradigms used to explore these phenomena.

Correct as is.   APA CODE: 2.10   INDEX NUMBER: 07

The group leader directed that all comments should be positive and that negative ideas should be rephrased as productive suggestions.

APA CODE: 2.11   INDEX NUMBER: 01

The judges could not distinguish between the children's drawings of human beings and the children's drawings of other species.

APA CODE: 2.11   INDEX NUMBER: 02

The experimenter administered either the drug or a placebo to each participant.

APA CODE: 2.11   INDEX NUMBER: 03

It is difficult not only for the computer to solve this problem but also for human beings to solve it.

APA CODE: 2.11   INDEX NUMBER: 04

The confederates were told that they should make the first choice, that they should use a neutral evaluation, and that they should avoid making eye contact with the participant.

APA CODE: 2.11   INDEX NUMBER: 05

Behavioral treatments were judged easier to administer by the therapists, while client-centered methods were judged more enjoyable by the clients.

APA CODE: 2.10   INDEX NUMBER: 05

Since there were no significant main effects or interactions involving experimenter, the data from the different experimenters were pooled.

APA CODE: 2.10   INDEX NUMBER: 06

Since the last edition of this text, there has been a major revision in the research paradigms used to explore these phenomena.

APA CODE: 2.10   INDEX NUMBER: 07

The group leader directed that all comments should be positive and negative ideas should be rephrased as productive suggestions.

APA CODE: 2.11   INDEX NUMBER: 01

The judges could not distinguish between the children's drawings of human beings and other species.

APA CODE: 2.11   INDEX NUMBER: 02

The experimenter either administered the drug or a placebo to each participant.

APA CODE: 2.11   INDEX NUMBER: 03

It is not only difficult for the computer to solve this problem but also for human beings to solve it.

APA CODE: 2.11   INDEX NUMBER: 04

The confederates were told that they should make the first choice, that they should use a neutral evaluation, and to avoid making eye contact with the participant.

APA CODE: 2.11   INDEX NUMBER: 05

Integrative Exercise: Grammar

Discussion

Whereas previous researchers have investigated the gender roles that children develop for their own behaviors, we monitored the gender-based schemata for the behavior of others that young children develop. As we predicted, the gender of the storyteller affected both the children's selection of the story to be read and their overt reponses during the reading. The children were more likely to choose stories with action verbs in the titles for the male storyteller to read than for the female storyteller to read. Furthermore, the children were more likely both to leave their seats and to interject comments while the male was reading than while the female was reading. We found the same effects in Experiment 1 with 4-year-olds and in Experiment 2 with 2-year-olds. There was no difference, in either age group, between the expectations exhibited by boys and the expectations exhibited by girls.

The data indicate that gender-role expectations develop at a younger age than had been indicated through the use of other response measures. Because neither the storyteller nor the books were familiar to any of the children, it seems reasonable to attribute the findings to a general role expectation rather than to specific experiences with the readers or with the stories. We can be sure that the expectations were the children's and not the observer's because the storyteller, as well as the books, was hidden from the children's observers. In addition, the storytellers' observers detected no differences in verbal or nonverbal cues for action and participation provided by the male and female storytellers whom we recruited and trained. The expectations seem to have wide generality, as the books that the children chose represented diverse topics and characters, and the behavioral differences in listening behaviors were not limited to the children who had selected the stories. As a further test of the generality of the phenomenon, we plan to use the same procedure to investigate children's gender-role expectations for other people of varying ages.

APA CODES: 2.06–2.12   INDEX NUMBER: 01

Integrative Exercise: Grammar

Discussion

While previous researchers have investigated the gender roles that children develop for their own behaviors, we monitored the gender-based schemas for the behavior of others which young children develop. As we predicted, the gender of the storyteller affects both the children's selection of the story to be read and their overt reponses during the reading. The children were more likely to choose stories with action verbs in the titles for the male storyteller to read than the female storyteller. Furthermore, the children were both more likely to leave their seats and to interject comments while the male was reading than while the female was reading. The same effects were found by us in Experiment 1 with 4-year-olds and in Experiment 2 with 2-year-olds. There was no difference between the expectations exhibited by boys and girls in either age group.

The data indicates that gender-role expectations develop at a younger age than had been indicated through the use of other response measures. Since neither the storyteller nor the books was familiar to any of the children, it seems reasonable to attribute the findings to a general role expectation rather than specific experiences with the readers or the stories. We can be sure that the expectations were the children's and not the observer's because the storyteller as well as the books were hidden from the children's observers. In addition, the storytellers' observers detected no differences in verbal or nonverbal cues for action and participation provided by the male and female storytellers who we recruited and trained. The expectations seem to have wide generality, as the books that the children chose represented diverse topics and characters, and the behavioral differences in listening behaviors were not limited to the children that had selected the stories. As a further test of the generality of the phenomenon, we plan to investigate children's gender-role expectations for other people of varying ages using the same procedure.

APA CODES: 2.06–2.12   INDEX NUMBER: 01

Guidelines to Reduce Bias in Language
APA Codes: 2.13–2.17

NOTES:

The participants were asked to think of their favorite teacher from elementary school and to rate her or him on the 20 evaluative dimensions.

APA CODE: 2.13   INDEX NUMBER: 01

The experimenter can decide when to provide the debriefing.

APA CODE: 2.13   INDEX NUMBER: 02

Typically, the department chair must give approval for each traineeship that is awarded.

APA CODE: 2.13   INDEX NUMBER: 03

The effects of social stimuli on eating have been investigated in the rat, monkey, and human.

APA CODE: 2.13   INDEX NUMBER: 04

The participants were 20 male students and 20 female students.

APA CODE: 2.13   INDEX NUMBER: 05

Each response was rated by a group of men and a group of women.

APA CODE: 2.13   INDEX NUMBER: 06

The participants were given descriptions of 12 pairs of husbands and wives and asked to predict the number of years each marriage would endure.

APA CODE: 2.13   INDEX NUMBER: 07

A psychological test battery was given to gay men and lesbians and to heterosexual men and women to determine whether there would be a relation between childhood sexual abuse and sexual identity.

APA CODE: 2.14   INDEX NUMBER: 01

Guidelines to Reduce Bias in Language
APA Codes: 2.13–2.17

These exercises give you practice in using nonsexist language and avoid ethnic bias (see the *Publication Manual*, sections 2.13–2.17). Mark corrections directly on the right-hand page and compare your responses with the correct answers on the left-hand page. When you are finished with this section, go on to the next section in which you need practice.

The participants were asked to think of their favorite teacher from elementary school and to rate her on the 20 evaluative dimensions.

APA CODE: 2.13   INDEX NUMBER: 01

The experimenter can decide when he should provide the debriefing.

APA CODE: 2.13   INDEX NUMBER: 02

Typically, the department chairman must give his approval for each traineeship that is awarded.

APA CODE: 2.13   INDEX NUMBER: 03

The effects of social stimuli on eating have been investigated in the rat, monkey, and man.

APA CODE: 2.13   INDEX NUMBER: 04

The participants were 20 male students and 20 coeds.

APA CODE: 2.13   INDEX NUMBER: 05

Each response was rated by a group of men and a group of females.

APA CODE: 2.13   INDEX NUMBER: 06

The participants were given descriptions of 12 men and their wives and asked to predict the number of years each marriage would endure.

APA CODE: 2.13   INDEX NUMBER: 07

A psychological test battery was given to gay men and women and to normal men and women to determine whether there would be a relation between childhood sexual abuse and sexual identity.

APA CODE: 2.14   INDEX NUMBER: 01

The expert judges classified the callers as Black, White, or Asian on the basis of voice characteristics. The researchers then determined the proportion of callers in each group who were urged to seek an abortion.

- *Note to students*: The *Publication Manual* offers guidance on what terms to use to refer to different racial and ethnic groups; it directs you to find out what the most acceptable term is and to use it in consideration of your readers. We followed the directions of the *Publication Manual* in arriving at the use of *Black*, *White*, and *Asian* in this example and at the terms we identified as correct in other exercises and test items in this instructional package. Because preferences and styles change over time, it is probably more important that you know to check for the most appropriate term than that the particular term you use in a given exercise or test item matches our judgment as to the most appropriate term.

APA CODE: 2.15   INDEX NUMBER: 01

An attempt was made to compare Native Americans who had been raised on reservations with Native Americans who had been raised in cities.

APA CODE: 2.15   INDEX NUMBER: 02

American children from Los Angeles and Russian children from Moscow were compared in terms of moral development and socialization.

APA CODE: 2.15   INDEX NUMBER: 03

Integrative Exercise: Guidelines to Reduce Bias in Language

College students were randomly assigned to same-sex or cross-sex dyads. After a Coca-Cola break they were asked to rate the etiquette of their partner. Female students rated female partners higher than they rated male partners. The male students in this study rated their female partners highly only when the female partners were not assertive (i.e., when they did not initiate social exchanges or change a topic of conversation). However, the lowest etiquette ratings were assigned by male students to other male students. Independent observations indicated that the male students were more assertive with other male students than with the female students but that the female students were more assertive with other female students than with male students.

APA CODES: 2.13–2.17   INDEX NUMBER: 01

The expert judges classified the callers as Negro, Caucasian, or Oriental on the basis of voice characteristics. The researchers then determined the proportion of callers in each group who were urged to seek an abortion.

APA CODE: 2.15   INDEX NUMBER: 01

An attempt was made to compare Indians who had been raised on reservations with Indians who had been raised in cities.

APA CODE: 2.15   INDEX NUMBER: 02

American children from Los Angeles and Communist children from Moscow were compared in terms of moral development and socialization.

APA CODE: 2.15   INDEX NUMBER: 03

Integrative Exercise: Guidelines to Reduce Bias in Language

College students were randomly assigned to same-sex or cross-sex dyads. After a Coca-Cola break they were asked to rate the etiquette of their partner. Coeds rated girl partners higher than they rated male partners. The men in this study rated the coeds highly only when the coeds were ladylike and not assertive (i.e., when they did not initiate social exchanges or change a topic of conversation). However, the lowest etiquette ratings were assigned by men to other guys. Independent observations indicated that the guys acted more masculine with other guys than with the gals but that the gals were more masculine with members of the gentle sex than with threatening men.

APA CODES: 2.13–2.17   INDEX NUMBER: 01

Punctuation and General Typing Instructions
APA Codes: 3.01–3.09, 5.11

NOTES:

All mathematics teachers know that word problems are more difficult for students to solve than are numerical problems. What the teachers do not know is how to teach students to solve word problems.

Correct as is.   APA CODE: 3.01   INDEX NUMBER: 01

The selection was translated from English into each of the other five languages. Native speakers of each language, who were also proficient in English, carried out the translations.

APA CODE: 3.01   INDEX NUMBER: 02

Speed of recovery after surgery was compared for patients who had a dog at home and for patients who had a cat at home. Patients who had both a dog and a cat were not included in the study.

APA CODE: 3.01   INDEX NUMBER: 03

Fathers who were single parents were expected to display greater androgyny than were fathers in dual-parent households. Androgyny was assessed by a standard inventory and by an activity checklist.

APA CODE: 3.01   INDEX NUMBER: 04

Average intelligence scores are a defining characteristic of dyslexia. Thus, it is impossible to compare empirically the intelligence of dyslexic and normal-reading children.

APA CODE: 3.01   INDEX NUMBER: 05

Punctuation and General Typing Instructions
APA Codes: 3.01–3.09, 5.11

These exercises cover the use of periods, commas, semicolons, colons, dashes, quotation marks, parentheses, and brackets, as well as correct spacing in typing (see the *Publication Manual*, sections 3.01–3.09 and 5.11). Mark corrections directly on the right-hand page, and compare your responses with the correct answers on the left-hand page. When you are finished with this section, go on to the next section in which you need practice.

All mathematics teachers know that word problems are more difficult for students to solve than are numerical problems. What the teachers do not know is how to teach students to solve word problems.

APA CODE: 3.01   INDEX NUMBER: 01

The selection was translated from English into each of the other five languages, native speakers of each language, who were also proficient in English, carried out the translations.

APA CODE: 3.01   INDEX NUMBER: 02

Speed of recovery after surgery was compared for patients who had a dog at home and for patients who had a cat at home: Patients who had both a dog and a cat were not included in the study.

APA CODE: 3.01   INDEX NUMBER: 03

Fathers who were single parents were expected to display greater androgyny than were fathers in dual-parent households, and androgyny was assessed by a standard inventory and by an activity checklist.

APA CODE: 3.01   INDEX NUMBER: 04

Average intelligence scores are a defining characteristic of dyslexia --Thus, it is impossible to compare empirically the intelligence of dyslexic and normal-reading children.

APA CODE: 3.01   INDEX NUMBER: 05

The child was seated at a table and given a variety of materials to use for the collage.

APA CODE: 3.02   INDEX NUMBER: 01

The independent variables were partner's gender, audience size, and criterion for success.

APA CODE: 3.02   INDEX NUMBER: 02

Any response that resulted in reward for the contingent participant also resulted in reward for the yoked partner.

APA CODE: 3.02   INDEX NUMBER: 03

The computer monitor displayed the training options, and the respondent selected one by pressing the corresponding key.

APA CODE: 3.02   INDEX NUMBER: 04

The confederate who was going to agree with the participant always spoke up before the confederate who was going to disagree with the participant.

APA CODE: 3.02   INDEX NUMBER: 05

The description of the assault, which was taken from an actual case, was identical for the respondents in all of the experimental conditions.

Correct as is.   APA CODE: 3.02   INDEX NUMBER: 06

The possibilities were suggested by Miller, Galanter, and Pribram (1960).

Correct as is.   APA CODE: 3.02   INDEX NUMBER: 07

The treatment was tested on clients who complained of phobias or addictions.

APA CODE: 3.02   INDEX NUMBER: 08

The team member who scored the highest on the preliminary task was the designated leader.

APA CODE: 3.02   INDEX NUMBER: 09

The child was seated at a table, and given a variety of materials to use for the collage.

APA CODE: 3.02   INDEX NUMBER: 01

The independent variables were partner's gender, audience size and criterion for success.

APA CODE: 3.02   INDEX NUMBER: 02

Any response, that resulted in reward for the contingent participant, also resulted in reward for the yoked partner.

APA CODE: 3.02   INDEX NUMBER: 03

The computer monitor displayed the training options and the respondent selected one by pressing the corresponding key.

APA CODE: 3.02   INDEX NUMBER: 04

The confederate, who was going to agree with the participant, always spoke up before the confederate, who was going to disagree with the participant.

APA CODE: 3.02   INDEX NUMBER: 05

The description of the assault, which was taken from an actual case, was identical for the respondents in all of the experimental conditions.

APA CODE: 3.02   INDEX NUMBER: 06

The possibilities were suggested by Miller, Galanter, and Pribram (1960).

APA CODE: 3.02   INDEX NUMBER: 07

The treatment was tested on clients who complained of phobias, or addictions.

APA CODE: 3.02   INDEX NUMBER: 08

The team member, who scored the highest on the preliminary task, was the designated leader.

APA CODE: 3.02   INDEX NUMBER: 09

Pupillary dilation was measured at the time of stimulus onset; heart rate was measured when the response was emitted.

APA CODE: 3.03   INDEX NUMBER: 01

Respondents were told that the occupations of the three people were newscaster, farmer, and accountant; teacher, plumber, and dentist; or optician, librarian, and welder.

APA CODE: 3.03   INDEX NUMBER: 02

The same speech confusions have been reported for bilingual children (Cardozo, 1984; Nakamura & Kato, 1978; Rivera, Mendez, & Avila, 1985).

Correct as is.

APA CODE: 3.03   INDEX NUMBER: 03

Expertise has been investigated in chess playing (Charness, 1981; Chase & Simon, 1973).

APA CODE: 3.03   INDEX NUMBER: 04

The essays that the first group read were student generated; those that the second group read were computer generated.

Correct as is.

APA CODE: 3.03   INDEX NUMBER: 05

The different methodologies have resulted in the same outcome: Constraining the alternatives results in faster solutions but poorer transfer.

APA CODE: 3.04   INDEX NUMBER: 01

For the three types of training, the proportions of new:old solutions were 1:3, 1:7, and 1:20, respectively.

Correct as is.

APA CODE: 3.04   INDEX NUMBER: 02

The order of preference for partners was as follows: adult-female, child-female, child-male, and adult-male.

APA CODE: 3.04   INDEX NUMBER: 03

Pupillary dilation was measured at the time of stimulus onset, heart rate was measured when the response was emitted.

APA CODE: 3.03   INDEX NUMBER: 01

Respondents were told that the occupations of the three people were newscaster, farmer, and accountant; teacher, plumber, and dentist; or optician, librarian, and welder.

APA CODE: 3.03   INDEX NUMBER: 02

The same speech confusions have been reported for bilingual children (Cardozo, 1984; Nakamura & Kato, 1978; Rivera, Mendez, & Avila, 1985).

APA CODE: 3.03   INDEX NUMBER: 03

Expertise has been investigated in chess playing (Charness, 1981; Chase & Simon, 1973).

APA CODE: 3.03   INDEX NUMBER: 04

The essays that the first group read were student generated; those that the second group read were computer generated.

APA CODE: 3.03   INDEX NUMBER: 05

The different methodologies have resulted in the same outcome--constraining the alternatives results in faster solutions but poorer transfer.

APA CODE: 3.04   INDEX NUMBER: 01

For the three types of training, the proportions of new:old solutions were 1:3, 1:7, and 1:20, respectively.

APA CODE: 3.04   INDEX NUMBER: 02

The order of preference for partners was as follows: Adult-female, child-female, child-male, and adult-male.

APA CODE: 3.04   INDEX NUMBER: 03

The different immigrant groups -- European Jews, Hispanic Catholics, and Asian Buddhists -- have displayed different forms of assimilation.

APA CODE: 3.05   INDEX NUMBER: 01

The participants rated their judgments on a 5-point scale ranging from *just guessing* to *absolutely certain.*

APA CODE: 3.06   INDEX NUMBER: 01

Respondents in the *gay* condition, who were told that the patient was gay, were more likely to diagnose the patients as having AIDS than were respondents who were not told that the patient was gay.

APA CODE: 3.06   INDEX NUMBER: 02

The term *multivariate analysis* is reserved for investigations that use multiple dependent variables.

APA CODE: 3.06   INDEX NUMBER: 03

An attempt was made to breed "vagabond" rats by inbreeding in each succeeding generation those rats that relocated their nests most frequently. Relocation behavior was assessed in each of 12 successive inbred generations of vagabond rats and control rats.

Correct as is.   APA CODE: 3.06   INDEX NUMBER: 04

The article by Brown and Kulik (1977), "Flashbulb Memories," contains reports of powerful naturalistic memories.

APA CODE: 3.06   INDEX NUMBER: 05

Garcia and Koelling (1966) demonstrated prepared learning.

APA CODE: 3.07   INDEX NUMBER: 01

Need achievement was assessed using the Thematic Apperception Test (TAT).

APA CODE: 3.07   INDEX NUMBER: 02

The different immigrant groups, European Jews, Hispanic Catholics, and Asian Buddhists, have displayed different forms of assimilation.

APA CODE: 3.05   INDEX NUMBER: 01

The participants rated their judgments on a 5-point scale ranging from "just guessing" to "absolutely certain."

APA CODE: 3.06   INDEX NUMBER: 01

Respondents in the "gay" condition, who were told that the patient was gay, were more likely to diagnose the patient as having AIDS than were respondents who were not told that the patient was gay.

APA CODE: 3.06   INDEX NUMBER: 02

The term "multivariate analysis" is reserved for investigations that use multiple dependent variables.

APA CODE: 3.06   INDEX NUMBER: 03

An attempt was made to breed "vagabond" rats by inbreeding in each succeeding generation those rats that relocated their nests most frequently. Relocation behavior was assessed in each of 12 successive inbred generations of vagabond rats and control rats.

APA CODE: 3.06   INDEX NUMBER: 04

The article by Brown and Kulik (1977), *Flashbulb Memories*, contains reports of powerful naturalistic memories.

APA CODE: 3.06   INDEX NUMBER: 05

Garcia and Koelling, 1966, demonstrated prepared learning.

APA CODE: 3.07   INDEX NUMBER: 01

Need achievement was assessed using the Thematic Apperception Test, TAT.

APA CODE: 3.07   INDEX NUMBER: 02

The distribution of reaction times was skewed. (Error responses, which accounted for less than 1% of the responses, were eliminated from this and all subsequent analyses.)

APA CODE: 3.07   INDEX NUMBER: 04

The three types of observers were (a) parents of the children being observed, (b) parents of matched children who were not being observed, and (c) childless adults who were matched on age with the parents of the children being observed.

APA CODE: 3.07   INDEX NUMBER: 05

(Brown, 1959, used a similar paradigm.)

Correct as is.

APA CODE: 3.08   INDEX NUMBER: 01

Students completed a demographic questionnaire, a personality test, or both.

APA CODE: 3.09   INDEX NUMBER: 01

Laboratory courses in psychology, even at the undergraduate level, cover a variety of substantive topics: learning, memory, cognition, social behavior, individual differences, and physiological psychology.

APA CODE: 5.11   INDEX NUMBER: 01

Person-to-person communication suffers different losses.

APA CODE: 5.11   INDEX NUMBER: 02

Although there was an effect for adolescent girls (see Table 1), the effect was greater for adolescent boys (see Table 2).

APA CODE: 5.11   INDEX NUMBER: 03

The distribution of reaction times was skewed. (Error responses, which accounted for less than 1% of the responses, were eliminated from this and all subsequent analyses).

APA CODE: 3.07   INDEX NUMBER: 04

The three types of observers were a: parents of the children being observed, b: parents of matched children who were not being observed, and c: childless adults who were matched on age with the parents of the children being observed.

APA CODE: 3.07   INDEX NUMBER: 05

(Brown, 1959, used a similar paradigm.)

APA CODE: 3.08   INDEX NUMBER: 01

Students completed a demographic questionnaire and/or a personality test.

APA CODE: 3.09   INDEX NUMBER: 01

Laboratory courses in psychology, even at the undergraduate level, cover a variety of substantive topics: learning, memory, cognition, social behavior, individual differences, and physiological psychology.

APA CODE: 5.11   INDEX NUMBER: 01

Person - to - person communication suffers different losses.

APA CODE: 5.11   INDEX NUMBER: 02

Although there was an effect for adolescent girls (see Table 1,) the effect was greater for adolescent boys (see Table 2).

APA CODE: 5.11   INDEX NUMBER: 03

Integrative Exercise: Punctuation and General Typing Instructions

Each participant performed three tasks — a memory-span test, an analogies test, and a syllogistic-reasoning test — during the experimental session. The memory-span task was presented orally, and the other two tasks were presented in written form. The memory task was always given first, followed by the analogies and reasoning tasks in counterbalanced order. Thus, the tasks were given in one of two orders: memory, analogies, and reasoning or memory, reasoning, and analogies. Four different contents were used for the tasks: abstract, "little-boy" thematic, "little-girl" thematic, and neutral thematic (on the basis of the ratings of topics in Experiment 1). Each participant received the same type of content for all four tasks. Different groups of male and female participants received the four different types of content. The participants were given unlimited time to perform each task; both latency and accuracy of response were recorded for each task. Variations in content were expected to affect performance on all three tasks and to affect the differences between the performance of men and women on the tasks.

APA CODES: 3.01–3.09, 5.11   INDEX NUMBER: 01

Integrative Exercise: Punctuation and General Typing Instructions

Each participant performed three tasks: a memory-span test, an analogies test and a syllogistic-reasoning test, during the experimental session. The memory-span task was presented orally; and the other two tasks were presented in written form. The memory task was always given first. Followed by the analogies and reasoning tasks in counterbalanced order. Thus, the tasks were given in one of two orders: memory, analogies, and reasoning: or memory, reasoning, and analogies. Four different contents were used for the tasks: abstract; *little-boy* thematic; *little-girl* thematic; and neutral thematic. (On the basis of the ratings of topics in Experiment 1.). Each participant received the same type of content for all four tasks. Different groups of male, and female, participants received the four different types of content. The participants were given unlimited time to perform each task--both latency and accuracy of response were recorded for each task. Variations in content were expected to affect performance on all three tasks, and to affect the differences between the performance of men and women on the tasks.

APA CODES: 3.01–3.09, 5.11   INDEX NUMBER: 01

NOTES:

Left - handed players were more accurate than right - handed players.

APA CODE: 3.11   INDEX NUMBER: 01

The program simulated the error - producing decisions of novices.

Correct as is.   APA CODE: 3.11   INDEX NUMBER: 02

Temporal groupings were more effective than spatial groupings.

APA CODE: 3.11   INDEX NUMBER: 03

A largely ignored illusion is now receiving attention from researchers.

APA CODE: 3.11   INDEX NUMBER: 04

Blood pressure readings were taken before and after each relaxation session.

APA CODE: 3.11   INDEX NUMBER: 05

The volunteers devoted time each day to skills relevant to job seeking.

APA CODE: 3.11   INDEX NUMBER: 06

The neighborhoods selected contained single - and double - family dwellings.

APA CODE: 3.11   INDEX NUMBER: 07

The experimental design allowed us to assess the effect of the pre test on performance.

APA CODE: 3.11   INDEX NUMBER: 08

An indirect measure of attitude or memory presents fewer opportunities for subjective bias than does self - report.

Correct as is.   APA CODE: 3.11   INDEX NUMBER: 09

Spelling and Hyphenation
APA Codes: 3.10–3.11

These exercises cover spelling and hyphenation (see the *Publication Manual*, sections 3.10–3.11). Mark corrections directly on the right-hand page, and compare your responses with the correct answers on the left-hand page. When you are finished with this section, go on to the next section in which you need practice.

Left handed players were more accurate than right handed players.

APA CODE: 3.11   INDEX NUMBER: 01

The program simulated the error producing decisions of novices.

APA CODE: 3.11   INDEX NUMBER: 02

Temporal groupings were more effective than spatial groupings.

APA CODE: 3.11   INDEX NUMBER: 03

A largely ignored illusion is now receiving attention from researchers.

APA CODE: 3.11   INDEX NUMBER: 04

Blood pressure readings were taken before and after each relaxation session.

APA CODE: 3.11   INDEX NUMBER: 05

The volunteers devoted time each day to skills relevant to job seeking.

APA CODE: 3.11   INDEX NUMBER: 06

The neighborhoods selected contained single and double family dwellings.

APA CODE: 3.11   INDEX NUMBER: 07

The experimental design allowed us to assess the effect of the pre test on performance.

APA CODE: 3.11   INDEX NUMBER: 08

An indirect measure of attitude or memory presents fewer opportunities for subjective bias than does self report.

APA CODE: 3.11   INDEX NUMBER: 09

Integrative Exercise: Spelling and Hyphenation

Memory for unusual foreign words and their English definitions as paired associates was improved using either the peg-word system or key-word system with imagery-arousing instructions. Other, more easily applied mnemonic systems such as the concrete-imagery or the action-imagery system were not tested. Same-sex pairs of sixth graders were randomly assigned to the experimental conditions. In a repeated measures design, children were provided with peg words and key words. Presentations were self-paced. Memory for the to-be-remembered vocabulary items was tested immediately and on a delayed post test.

APA CODES: 3.10–3.11 INDEX NUMBER: 01

Integrative Exercise: Spelling and Hyphenation

Memory for unusual foreign words and their English definitions as paired-associates was improved using either the peg word system or key-word system with imagery-arousing instructions. Other, more-easily applied mnemonic systems such as the concrete imagery or the action-imagery system were not tested. Same-sex pairs of sixth-graders were randomly assigned to the experimental conditions. In a repeated-measures design, children were provided with peg-words and key-words. Presentations were self paced. Memory for the to be remembered vocabulary items was tested immediately and on a delayed post-test.

APA CODES: 3.10–3.11   INDEX NUMBER: 01

Capitalization and General Typing Instructions
APA Codes: 3.12–3.18, 5.09

NOTES:

Research supports one conclusion: Cockroaches will avoid or escape bright light.

APA CODE: 3.12   INDEX NUMBER: 01

In an article by Pyro and Mani, "A Theory of Firesetting in Children and Adolescents," the authors suggested that firesetting should be studied as a legitimate problem in its own right.

APA CODE: 3.13   INDEX NUMBER: 01

The author suggests that Freudian slips can be a symptom of a neurological disorder.

Correct as is.   APA CODE: 3.14   INDEX NUMBER: 01

The theory of intrinsic job satisfaction of Hackman and Oldham (1980) describes principles of job redesign.

APA CODE: 3.14   INDEX NUMBER: 02

A Sony 2400 portable videocamera was used to record the nonverbal behaviors of students in the love-lie and used-car-lie conditions.

APA CODE: 3.14   INDEX NUMBER: 03

Social Distance

2

Abstract

In past research, it has been observed that strangers walk closer to physically healthy than to physically impaired persons.

Correct as is.   APA CODE: 5.09   INDEX NUMBER: 01

Capitalization and General Typing Instructions
APA Codes: 3.12–3.18, 5.09

These exercises cover the capitalization of (a) words beginning a sentence; (b) major words in titles and headings; (c) proper nouns and trade names; (d) nouns followed by numbers or letters; (e) titles of tests; (f) names of conditions or groups in an experiment; and (g) names of factors, variables, and effects (see the *Publication Manual*, sections 3.12–3.18 and 5.09). Mark corrections directly on the right-hand page, and compare your responses with the correct answers on the left-hand page. When you are finished with this section, go on to the next section in which you need practice.

Research supports one conclusion: cockroaches will avoid or escape bright light.

APA CODE: 3.12   INDEX NUMBER: 01

In an article by Pyro and Mani, "A theory of firesetting in children and adolescents," the authors suggested that firesetting should be studied as a legitimate problem in its own right.

APA CODE: 3.13   INDEX NUMBER: 01

The author suggests that Freudian slips can be a symptom of a neurological disorder.

APA CODE: 3.14   INDEX NUMBER: 01

The Theory of Intrinsic Job Satisfaction of Hackman and Oldham (1980) describes principles of job redesign.

APA CODE: 3.14   INDEX NUMBER: 02

A sony 2400 portable videocamera was used to record the nonverbal behaviors of students in the love-lie and used-car-lie conditions.

APA CODE: 3.14   INDEX NUMBER: 03

Social Distance

2

Abstract

In past research, it has been observed that strangers walk closer to physically healthy than to physically impaired persons.

APA CODE: 5.09   INDEX NUMBER: 01

Integrative Exercise: Capitalization and General Typing Instructions

Deudodder (1999), in his article "Time Vacuum Effects and Procrastination in College Students," claimed that many college students suffer from a form of jet lag. In the three studies he reported, Deudodder showed how the typical college student disrupts his or her circadian rhythm without flying on a jet. His "all-nighter-napper" theory suggests that jet lag is produced when students stay awake all night (studying or partying) and then nap the entire following day. To test his theory, he conducted four experiments. In Experiment 1, he asked students from psychology courses to complete the Deudodder Intrazone Time Inventory.

APA CODES: 3.12–3.18, 5.09   INDEX NUMBER: 01

Integrative Exercise: Capitalization and General Typing Instructions

Deudodder (1999), in his article "Time vacuum effects and procrastination in college students," claimed that many College students suffer from a form of Jet Lag. In the three studies he reported, Deudodder showed how the typical college student disrupts his or her Circadian rhythm without flying on a jet. His "All-Nighter-Napper" theory suggests that Jet Lag is produced when students stay awake all night (studying or partying) and then nap the entire following day. To test his theory, he conducted four experiments. In experiment 1, he asked students from Psychology courses to complete the Deudodder intrazone time inventory.

APA CODES: 3.12–3.18, 5.09   INDEX NUMBER: 01

Italics
APA Code: 3.19

NOTES:

Kelley, in his article in the *American Psychologist*, described three dimensions of causal attribution.

APA CODE: 3.19   INDEX NUMBER: 01

Fabricated legal descriptions, called *case facts*, were presented to mock juries; however, *case facts* were not presented to shadow juries.

APA CODE: 3.19   INDEX NUMBER: 02

Children who were low achievers and had low socioeconomic status were rated significantly less competent by their teachers, F(2, 14) = 7.47, p < .001.

APA CODE: 3.19   INDEX NUMBER: 03

Adults who were sensitive to $NaCl$ were also more likely to have hypertension.

APA CODE: 3.19   INDEX NUMBER: 04

Genetic theories of psychopathology such as the diathesis stress model suggest that schizophrenia may be predisposed by genetic structures but will not appear *without* a stressful environment.

APA CODE: 3.19   INDEX NUMBER: 05

Integrative Exercise: Italics

A temperature discrimination task was presented to human beings (*Homo sapiens*) and crickets (*Gryllidae*). Then, just noticeable differences (*JND*s) were determined for each species. The *JND*s for crickets were *smaller*, as indicated by a *t* test, than those for human beings.

APA CODE: 3.19   INDEX NUMBER: 01

Italics
APA Code: 3.19

These exercises cover the use of italics (see the *Publication Manual*, section 3.19). Mark corrections directly on the right-hand page, and compare your responses with the correct answers on the left-hand page. When you are finished with this section, go on to the next section in which you need practice.

Kelley, in his article in the American Psychologist, described three dimensions of causal attribution.

APA CODE: 3.19   INDEX NUMBER: 01

Fabricated legal descriptions, called case facts, were presented to mock juries; however, case facts were not presented to shadow juries.

APA CODE: 3.19   INDEX NUMBER: 02

Children who were low achievers and had low socioeconomic status were rated significantly less competent by their teachers, F(2, 14) = 7.47, p < .001.

APA CODE: 3.19   INDEX NUMBER: 03

Adults who were sensitive to NaCl were also more likely to have hypertension.

APA CODE: 3.19   INDEX NUMBER: 04

Genetic theories of psychopathology such as the diathesis stress model suggest that schizophrenia may be predisposed by genetic structures but will not appear without a stressful environment.

APA CODE: 3.19   INDEX NUMBER: 05

Integrative Exercise: Italics

A temperature discrimination task was presented to human beings (*Homo sapiens*) and crickets (Gryllidae). Then, just noticeable differences (*JND*s) were determined for each species. The *JND*s for crickets were *smaller*, as indicated by a t test, than those for human beings.

APA CODE: 3.19   INDEX NUMBER: 01

Abbreviations
APA Codes: 3.20–3.29

NOTES:

According to Sternberg (1985), current measures of IQ do not reflect the triarchic nature of human intelligence.

Correct as is.   APA CODE: 3.22   INDEX NUMBER: 01

When the experimenter delivered the conditioned stimulus (CS), the pigeon pecked the key and avoided being drenched in cold water.

APA CODE: 3.23   INDEX NUMBER: 01

The reaction time (RT) was recorded after each dolphin received two clicks. The RT was not recorded when killer whales were within sonar range.

Correct as is.   APA CODE: 3.23   INDEX NUMBER: 02

Participatory management (e.g., shared goal-setting and mutual evaluation) was more effective in the smaller organizations (i.e., those with fewer than 100 workers).

APA CODE: 3.24   INDEX NUMBER: 01

Not all traditional sex role expectancies (e.g., women may cry, men should not cry) transfer into all organizational cultures (i.e., an organization's social environment). Some organizations punish traditional sex role behavior in women but not in men (e.g., military or industrial organizations).

APA CODE: 3.24   INDEX NUMBER: 02

Abbreviations
APA Codes: 3.20–3.29

These exercises cover the use of abbreviations, explanation of abbreviations, abbreviations accepted as words, abbreviations used often in APA journals, abbreviations of units of measurement and statistics, use of periods with abbreviations, plurals of abbreviations, and abbreviations beginning a sentence (see the *Publication Manual*, sections 3.20–3.29). Mark corrections directly on the right-hand page, and compare your responses with the correct answers on the left-hand page. When you are finished with this section, go on to the next section in which you need practice.

According to Sternberg (1985), current measures of IQ do not reflect the triarchic nature of human intelligence.

APA CODE: 3.22   INDEX NUMBER: 01

When the E delivered the CS, the pigeon pecked the key and avoided being drenched in cold water.

APA CODE: 3.23   INDEX NUMBER: 01

The reaction time (RT) was recorded after each dolphin received two clicks. The RT was not recorded when killer whales were within sonar range.

APA CODE: 3.23   INDEX NUMBER: 02

Participatory management (for example, shared goal-setting and mutual evaluation) was more effective in the smaller organizations (i.e., those with fewer than 100 workers).

APA CODE: 3.24   INDEX NUMBER: 01

Not all traditional sex role expectancies e.g., women may cry, men should not cry, transfer into all organizational cultures (i.e., an organization's social environment). Some organizations punish traditional sex role behavior in women but not in men (e.g., military or industrial organizations).

APA CODE: 3.24   INDEX NUMBER: 02

It took the respondents 20 s to 2 min to recall the stimulus word. After a 3-hr delay, respondents began the trials again.

APA CODE: 3.25   INDEX NUMBER: 01

Integrative Exercise: Abbreviations

Fewer abbreviation identification errors were made by readers of papers about learning and memory written in APA style than in any other writing style. Abbreviations such as intertrial interval (ITI), conditioned stimulus (CS), and short-term memory (STM) were correctly identified by BS and BA students alike regardless of their IQs.

- *Note to students:* Many of you probably knew that the abbreviations ITI, CS, and STM given in the draft version should have been defined on first use. However, you may not have known what all of the abbreviations stood for, so you could not provide the complete correction. We could think of no better way to make the point that abbreviations must be defined for the reader.

APA CODES: 3.20–3.29   INDEX NUMBER: 01

It took the respondents 20 seconds to 2 minutes to recall the stimulus word. After a 3-hour delay, respondents began the trials again.

APA CODE: 3.25   INDEX NUMBER: 01

Integrative Exercise: Abbreviations

Fewer abbreviation identification errors were made by readers of papers about learning and memory written in APA style than in any other writing style. Abbreviations such as ITI, CS, and STM were correctly identified by B.S. and B.A. students alike regardless of their intelligence quotients (IQs).

APA CODES: 3.20–3.29   INDEX NUMBER: 01

Headings and Series and General Typing Instructions
APA Codes: 3.30–3.33, 5.10, 5.12

NOTES:

The Social Psychology of Rumors

Disaster Rumors

Conflict Rumors

Wish Rumors

Emotions and Rumor Transmission

References

The Social Psychology of Rumors

Wish Rumors

Dread Rumors

   Disease rumors.

   Disaster rumors.

   Invasion rumors.

Conclusion

References

The adolescents were divided into 18 groups according to whether they selected a role model who was (a) Black, White, or Cuban; (b) male or female; and (c) an athlete, entertainer, or scientist.

Headings and Series and General Typing Instructions
APA Codes: 3.30–3.33, 5.10, 5.12

This group of exercises will help you learn to organize a manuscript with headings, to select the levels of headings, and to clearly present series (see the *Publication Manual*, sections 3.30–3.33, 5.10, and 5.12). Mark corrections directly on the right-hand page, and compare your responses with the correct answers on the left-hand page. When you are finished with this section, go on to the next section in which you need practice.

Introduction

The Social Psychology of Rumors

Disaster Rumors

Conflict Rumors

Wish Rumors

Emotions and Rumor Transmission

References

APA CODES: 3.30, 5.10   INDEX NUMBER: 01

The Social Psychology of Rumors

Wish Rumors

Dread Rumors

  Disease rumors.

  Disaster rumors.

  Invasion rumors.

Conclusion

References

APA CODES: 3.30–3.32, 5.10   INDEX NUMBER: 02

The adolescents were divided into 18 groups according to whether they selected a role model who was (1) Black, White, or Cuban, (2) male or female, and (3) an athlete, entertainer, or scientist.

APA CODE: 3.33   INDEX NUMBER: 01

Preliminary Measures

Sociability.

APA CODE: 5.10   INDEX NUMBER: 01

Integrative Exercise: Headings and Series and General Typing Instructions

IRRATIONAL FEAR

Fear of Living Organisms

Amphibian Phobias

Fear of Salamanders

Forest newt phobia. There is a salamander found near Salamanca, New York, a tiny pink and white forest newt, that has been shown to arouse tremendous fear in people who already have (a) a spaghetti phobia, (b) a worm phobia, and (c) mysophobia.

APA CODES: 3.30–3.33, 5.10, 5.12   INDEX NUMBER: 01

Social Skills Training

Sociability.

APA CODE: 5.10   INDEX NUMBER: 01

Integrative Exercise: Headings and Series and General Typing Instructions

Irrational fear

Fear of Living Organisms

AMPHIBIAN PHOBIAS

Fear of salamanders

Forest newt phobia. There is a salamander found near Salamanca, New York, a tiny pink and white forest newt, that has been shown to arouse tremendous fear in people who already have (1) a spaghetti phobia, (2) a worm phobia, and (3) mysophobia.

APA CODES: 3.30–3.33, 5.10, 5.12   INDEX NUMBER: 01

NOTES:

Dykens and Gerrard (1986) concluded that the psychological profile of bulimics and repeat dieters is similar:

> It appears that both repeat dieters and bulimics can be characterized as having low self-esteem and an external locus of control. This profile supports suggestions from case studies that women with eating disorders suffer from feelings of ineffectiveness and lack of control over life decisions. (p. 288)

APA CODES: 3.34 & 3.39   INDEX NUMBER: 01

The author speculated that "negative exemplars within the self-concept are more confidently known than affirmative exemplars" (Brinthaup, 1983, p. 52).

Correct as is.   APA CODES: 3.34 & 3.39   INDEX NUMBER: 02

One college student interviewed said, "Campus 'lingo' is not just language, it is a fence to hold in friends and keep out geeks."

APA CODE: 3.36   INDEX NUMBER: 01

"Four score and seven years ago our fathers brought forth upon this continent a new nation ... dedicated to the proposition that all men are created equal."

APA CODE: 3.38   INDEX NUMBER: 01

Quotations and General Typing Instructions
APA Codes: 3.34–3.41, 5.13

These exercises cover quoting sources, accuracy, double versus single quotation marks, changes from the source requiring no explanation, changes from the source requiring explanation, citation of sources, and permission to quote (see the *Publication Manual*, sections 3.34–3.41 and 5.13). Mark corrections directly on the right-hand page, and compare your responses with the correct answers on the left-hand page. When you are finished with this section, go on to the next section in which you need practice.

Dykens and Gerrard (1986, p. 288) concluded that the psychological profile of bulimics and repeat dieters is similar: "It appears that both repeat dieters and bulimics can be characterized as having low self-esteem and an external locus of control. This profile supports suggestions from case studies that women with eating disorders suffer from feelings of ineffectiveness and lack of control over life decisions."

APA CODES: 3.34 & 3.39   INDEX NUMBER: 01

The author speculated that "negative exemplars within the self-concept are more confidently known than affirmative exemplars" (Brinthaup, 1983, p. 52).

APA CODES: 3.34 & 3.39   INDEX NUMBER: 02

One college student interviewed said, "Campus 'lingo' is not just another language, it is a fence to hold in friends and keep out geeks."

APA CODE: 3.36   INDEX NUMBER: 01

"Four score and seven years ago our fathers brought forth upon this continent a new nation.... dedicated to the proposition that all men are created equal."

APA CODE: 3.38   INDEX NUMBER: 01

These investigators suggested that "although state and trait anxiety appear to have a similar effect on rumor transmission, it cannot be concluded that this effect was produced by similar social processes" (Walker & Beckerle, 1987, p. 358).

Correct as is.   APA CODE: 3.39   INDEX NUMBER: 01

The respondent asked, "Is this my or her heartbeat I am hearing?" The experimenter replied, "It is not yours or hers!"

Correct as is.   APA CODE: 5.13   INDEX NUMBER: 01

Integrative Exercise: Quotations and General Typing Instructions

Duerf (1990) suggested that "the 'subliminal guilt effect' happens only when semi-nude images are subtly inscribed on the labels of whiskey bottles of light drinkers" (p. 68). Duerf concluded the following:

> Some light drinkers have a negative oral fixation which inhibits their pursuit of oral pleasure. One ounce of alcohol from the forbidden bottle apparently releases a flood of libido associated with the mouth *and* the genitals. Oral guilt enters through the front door and sexual guilt sneaks in the back like an *uninvited* [italics added] guest. (p. 101)

APA CODES: 3.34–3.41, 5.13   INDEX NUMBER: 01

These investigators suggested that "although state and trait anxiety appear to have a similar effect on rumor transmission, it cannot be concluded that this effect was produced by similar social processes" (Walker & Beckerle, 1987, p. 358).

APA CODE: 3.39   INDEX NUMBER: 01

The respondent asked, "Is this my or her heartbeat I am hearing?" The experimenter replied, "It is not yours or hers!"

APA CODE: 5.13   INDEX NUMBER: 01

Integrative Exercise: Quotations and General Typing Instructions

Duerf (1990) suggested that "the "subliminal guilt effect" happens only when semi-nude images are subtly inscribed on the labels of whiskey bottles of light drinkers (p. 68)".

Duerf concluded the following:

> Some light drinkers have a negative oral fixation which inhibits their pursuit of oral pleasure. One ounce of alcohol from the forbidden bottle apparently releases a flood of libido associated with the mouth *and* the genitals. Oral guilt enters through the front door and sexual guilt sneaks in the back like an *uninvited* [italics added] guest. (page 101)

APA CODES: 3.34–3.41, 5.13   INDEX NUMBER: 01

NOTES:

The concept of chunking was introduced by Miller (1956).

APA CODE: 3.94   INDEX NUMBER: 01

Other authors focus on the role of affect (Zajonc, 1984).

APA CODE: 3.94   INDEX NUMBER: 02

Sternberg (1966) was the first to report the effect of target set size on reaction time. Sternberg used target sets of size 1, 2, or 4.

APA CODE: 3.94   INDEX NUMBER: 03

Garcia and Koelling (1966) demonstrated that rats could learn aversions to specific flavors with minimal training. To do so, Garcia and Koelling exposed rats to noxious radiation shortly after they drank water with a distinctive flavor.

APA CODE: 3.95   INDEX NUMBER: 01

Kahn, Staerk, and Bonk (1974) used biofeedback to treat asthma, and Gamble and Elder (1983) used it to reduce muscle tension. In addition to biofeedback, Kahn et al. used a form of classical conditioning.

Correct as is.

APA CODE: 3.95   INDEX NUMBER: 02

Reference Citations in Text
APA Codes: 3.94–3.103

These exercises give you practice in citing in text works by a single author, by two or more authors, by corporate authors, with no author or with an anonymous author, by authors with the same surname, and by two or more authors within the same set of parentheses; specific parts of a source; personal communications; references to legal materials; and references in parenthetical material (see the *Publication Manual*, sections 3.94–3.103). Mark corrections directly on the right-hand page, and compare your responses with the correct answers on the left-hand page. When you are finished with this section, go on to the next section in which you need practice.

The concept of chunking was introduced by Miller (Miller, 1956).

APA CODE: 3.94   INDEX NUMBER: 01

Other authors focus on the role of affect (Zajonc, *American Psychologist*, 1984).

APA CODE: 3.94   INDEX NUMBER: 02

Sternberg (1966) was the first to report the effect of target set size on reaction time. Sternberg (1966) used target sets of size 1, 2, or 4.

APA CODE: 3.94   INDEX NUMBER: 03

Garcia and Koelling (1966) demonstrated that rats could learn aversions to specific flavors with minimal training. To do so, Garcia, et al. exposed rats to noxious radiation shortly after they drank water with a distinctive flavor.

APA CODE: 3.95   INDEX NUMBER: 01

Kahn, Staerk, and Bonk (1974) used biofeedback to treat asthma, and Gamble and Elder (1983) used it to reduce muscle tension. In addition to biofeedback, Kahn et al. used a form of classical conditioning.

APA CODE: 3.95   INDEX NUMBER: 02

Diaz-Guerrero, Reyes-Lagunes, Witzke, and Holtzman (1976) investigated the effects of TV in a different culture. Diaz-Guerrero et al. used an experimental design with randomization to demonstrate the effectiveness of watching "Sesame Street" among Mexican preschool children.

APA CODE: 3.95   INDEX NUMBER: 03

Best et al. (1977) found similar gender stereotypes among boys and girls in the United States.

APA CODE: 3.95   INDEX NUMBER: 04

Changes in the delusions of Chinese schizophrenic patients have accompanied changes in Chinese society (Yu-Fen & Neng, 1981).

APA CODE: 3.95   INDEX NUMBER: 05

One example of computer simulation of human problem-solving performance is the General Problem-Solver (Newell, Shaw, & Simon, 1959; Newell & Simon, 1961, 1972).

APA CODE: 3.99   INDEX NUMBER: 01

Contemporary approaches (Kamin, 1969; Rescorla, 1966) focus on the role of informational variables and cognitive processes in classical conditioning.

APA CODE: 3.99   INDEX NUMBER: 02

Postulates 1 and 2 (Hull, 1943, p. 47) specify the neural effects of external stimuli.

APA CODE: 3.101   INDEX NUMBER: 01

Although cats, dogs, and mice do not show the same kind of biased laterality in paw preference as humans do in handedness, song birds do show a pattern of asymmetry in brain control of song that is similar to the pattern of brain control of speech in humans (Springer & Deutsch, 1981, chap. 8).

APA CODE: 3.101   INDEX NUMBER: 02

Diaz-Guerrero, Reyes-Lagunes, Witzke, and Holtzman (Diaz-Guerrero et al., 1976) investigated the effects of TV in a different culture. Diaz-Guerrero, Reyes-Lagunes, Witzke, and Holtzman used an experimental design with randomization to demonstrate the effectiveness of watching "Sesame Street" among Mexican preschool children.

APA CODE: 3.95   INDEX NUMBER: 03

Best, Williams, Cloud, Davis, Robertson, Edwards, Giles, and Fowles (1977) found similar gender stereotypes among boys and girls in the United States.

APA CODE: 3.95   INDEX NUMBER: 04

Changes in the delusions of Chinese schizophrenic patients have accompanied changes in Chinese society (Yu-Fen and Neng, 1981).

APA CODE: 3.95   INDEX NUMBER: 05

One example of computer simulation of human problem-solving performance is the General Problem-Solver (Newell, Shaw, & Simon, 1959; Newell & Simon, 1961; Newell & Simon, 1972).

APA CODE: 3.99   INDEX NUMBER: 01

Contemporary approaches (Rescorla, 1966; Kamin, 1969) focus on the role of informational variables and cognitive processes in classical conditioning.

APA CODE: 3.99   INDEX NUMBER: 02

Postulates 1 and 2 (p. 47, Hull, 1943) specify the neural effects of external stimuli.

APA CODE: 3.101   INDEX NUMBER: 01

Although cats, dogs, and mice do not show the same kind of biased laterality in paw preference as humans do in handedness, song birds to show a pattern of asymmetry in brain control of song that is similar to the pattern of brain control of speech in humans (Springer & Deutsch, 1981) (Chapter 8).

APA CODE: 3.101   INDEX NUMBER: 02

Integrative Exercise: Reference Citations in Text

Holmes and Rahe (1967) argued that change, especially major change, causes stress. Boyce et al. (1977) found that stress mediated by life events reduces resistance to respiratory infections. Other researchers (Lazarus, 1980) have focused on the more mundane stresses, or "hassles," in daily life as predictors of illness and depression. The person's evaluation of the event, as much as the nature of the event itself, affects the degree to which an event is experienced as stressful (Lazarus, 1966, 1968; Lazarus & Launier, 1978; Lazarus, Speisman, Davison, & Mordkiff, 1964).

Numerous techniques have been developed to help people cope with stress. Progressive relaxation (e.g., Jacob, Kraemer, & Agras, 1977) and biofeedback (e.g., Yates, 1980) have been used to control arousal. Jacob et al. found that progressive relaxation reduced high blood pressure. The critical role of cognitive appraisal in stress underlies stress management programs (Meichenbaum & Jaremko, 1983; Meichenbaum & Turk, 1982). Meichenbaum and Turk had participants plan ahead and develop strategies for dealing with stressful situations.

APA CODES: 3.93–3.103   INDEX NUMBER: 01

Integrative Exercise: Reference Citations in Text

Holmes and Rahe (Holmes & Rahe, 1967) argued that change, especially major change, causes stress. Boyce, Jensen, Cassel, Collier, Smith, and Ramey (1977) found that stress mediated by life events reduces resistance to respiratory infections. Other researchers (Lazarus, 1980) have focused on the more mundane stresses, or "hassles," in daily life as predictors of illness and depression. The person's evaluation of the event, as much as the nature of the event itself, affects the degree to which an event is experienced as stressful (Lazarus, Speisman, Davison, & Mordkiff, 1964; Lazarus, 1966; Lazarus, 1968; Lazarus & Launier, 1978).

Numerous techniques have been developed to help people cope with stress. Progressive relaxation (e.g., Jacob, Kraemer and Agras, 1977) and biofeedback (e.g., Yates, 1980) have been used to control arousal. Jacob, Kraemer, and Agras found that progressive relaxation reduced high blood pressure. The critical role of cognitive appraisal in stress underlies stress management programs (Meichenbaum & Jaremko, 1983; Meichenbaum & Turk, 1982). Meichenbaum et al. (1982) had participants plan ahead and develop strategies for dealing with stressful situations.

APA CODES: 3.94–3.103   INDEX NUMBER: 01

NOTES:

Hirsch, H. V. B., & Spinelli, D. N. (1970). Visual experience modifies distribution of horizontally and vertically oriented receptive fields of cats. *Science, 168,* 869-871.

Hirsch, H. V. B., & Spinelli, D. N. (1971). Modification of the distribution of receptive field orientation in cats by selective visual exposure during development. *Experimental Brain Research, 13,* 509-527.

APA CODE: 4.04   INDEX NUMBER: 01

Premack, D. (1963a). Predictions of the comparative reinforcement values of running and drinking. *Science, 139,* 1062-1063.

Premack, D. (1963b). Rate differential reinforcement in monkey manipulation. *Journal of the Experimental Analysis of Behavior, 6,* 81-89.

APA CODE: 4.04   INDEX NUMBER: 02

Gibson, E. J. (1984). Perceptual development from the ecological approach. In M. E. Lamb, A. L. Brown, & B. Rogoff (Eds.), *Advances in developmental psychology* (Vol. 3, pp. 243-285). Hillsdale, NJ: Erlbaum.

Gibson, J. J. (1979). *The ecological approach to perception.* Boston: Houghton Mifflin.

Correct as is.

APA CODE: 4.04   INDEX NUMBER: 03

Reference List and Typing the Parts of a Manuscript
APA Codes: 4.01–4.05, 5.18, Appendix D

These exercises cover agreement of text with the reference list, construction of an accurate and complete reference list, APA reference style, references to legal materials, the order of references in the reference list, and applying APA reference style (see the *Publication Manual*, sections 4.01–4.05, and 5.18, Appendix D). Mark corrections directly on the right-hand page, and compare your responses with the correct answers on the left-hand page. When you are finished with this section, you are ready to take the practice test.

Hirsch, H. V. B., & Spinelli, D. N. (1971). Modification of the distribution of receptive field orientation in cats by selective visual exposure during development. *Experimental Brain Research, 13,* 509-527.

Hirsch, H. V. B., & Spinelli, D. N. (1970). Visual experience modifies distribution of horizontally and vertically oriented receptive fields of cats. *Science, 168,* 869-871.

APA CODE: 4.04   INDEX NUMBER: 01

Premack, D. (1963). Rate differential reinforcement in monkey manipulation. *Journal of the Experimental Analysis of Behavior, 6,* 81-89.

Premack, D. (1963). Predictions of the comparative reinforcement values of running and drinking. *Science, 139,* 1062-1063.

APA CODE: 4.04   INDEX NUMBER: 02

Gibson, E. J. (1984). Perceptual development from the ecological approach. In M. E. Lamb, A. L. Brown, & B. Rogoff (Eds.), *Advances in developmental psychology* (Vol. 3, pp. 243-285). Hillsdale, NJ: Erlbaum.

Gibson, J. J. (1979). *The ecological approach to perception.* Boston: Houghton Mifflin.

APA CODE: 4.04   INDEX NUMBER: 03

Mahoney, M. J. (1977). Some applied issues in self-monitoring. In J. D. Cone & R. P. Hawkins (Eds.), *Behavioral assessment: New directions in clinical psychology* (pp. 241-254). New York: Brunner/Mazel.

Mahoney, M. J., Moore, B. S., Wade, T. C., & Moura, N. G. M. (1973). The effects of continuous and intermittent self-monitoring on academic behavior. *Journal of Consulting and Clinical Psychology, 41*, 65-69.

Mahoney, M. J., Moura, N. M., & Wade, T. C. (1973). The relative efficacy of self-reward, self-punishment, and self-monitoring techniques for weight loss. *Journal of Consulting and Clinical Psychology, 40*, 404-407.

APA CODE: 4.04   INDEX NUMBER: 04

Balagura, S. (1968). Influence of osmotic and caloric loads upon lateral hypothalamic self-stimulation. *Journal of Comparative and Physiological Psychology, 66*, 325-328.

APA CODE: 4.16   INDEX NUMBER: 01

Hraba, J., & Grant, G. (1970). Black is beautiful: A reexamination of racial preference and identification. *Journal of Personality and Social Psychology, 16*, 398-402.

APA CODE: 4.16   INDEX NUMBER: 02

Peterson, S. E., Fox, P. T., Posner, M. I., Mintun, W., & Raichle, M. E. (1988). Positron emission tomographic studies of the cortical anatomy of single word processing. *Nature, 331*, 585-589.

APA CODE: 4.16   INDEX NUMBER: 03

Zafiropoulou, M., & McPherson, F. M. (1980). "Preparedness" and the severity and outcome of clinical phobias. *Behavior Research and Therapy, 24*, 221-222.

APA CODE: 4.16   INDEX NUMBER: 04

Mahoney, M. J., Moura, N. M., & Wade, T. C. (1973). The relative efficacy of self-reward, self-punishment, and self-monitoring techniques for weight loss. *Journal of Consulting and Clinical Psychology, 40,* 404-407.

Mahoney, M. J., Moore, B. S., Wade, T. C., & Moura, N. G. M. (1973). The effects of continuous and intermittent self-monitoring on academic behavior. *Journal of Consulting and Clinical Psychology, 41,* 65-69.

Mahoney, M. J. (1977). Some applied issues in self-monitoring. In J. D. Cone & R. P. Hawkins (Eds.), *Behavioral assessment: New directions in clinical psychology* (pp. 241-254). New York: Brunner/Mazel.

APA CODE: 4.04   INDEX NUMBER: 04

Balagura, S. (1968). "Influence of Osmotic and Caloric Loads Upon Lateral Hypothalamic Self-Stimulation." *Journal of Comparative and Physiological Psychology, 66,* 325-328.

APA CODE: 4.16   INDEX NUMBER: 01

J. Hraba and G. Grant. (1970). Black is beautiful: A reexamination of racial preference and identification. *Journal of Personality and Social Psychology, 16,* 398-402.

APA CODE: 4.16   INDEX NUMBER: 02

Peterson, S. E., Fox, P. T., Posner, M. I., Mintun, W., & Raichle, M. E. (1988). Positron emission tomographic studies of the cortical anatomy of single word processing. *Nature, 331,* pp. 585-589.

APA CODE: 4.16   INDEX NUMBER: 03

Zafiropoulou, M., & McPherson, F. M. "Preparedness" and the severity and outcome of clinical phobias. *Behavior Research and Therapy,* 1980, 24, 221-222.

APA CODE: 4.16   INDEX NUMBER: 04

Klatzky, R. L. (1980). *Human memory: Structures and processes* (2nd ed.). San Francisco: Freeman.

APA CODE: 4.16   INDEX NUMBER: 05

Yamamoto, T., Yayama, N., & Kawamura, Y. (1981). Central processing of taste perception. In Y. Katsuki, R. Norgren, & M. Sato (Eds.), *Brain mechanisms of sensation* (pp. 197-208). New York: Wiley.

APA CODE: 4.16   INDEX NUMBER: 06

Squire, L. R., & Cohen, N. J. (1982). Remote memory, retrograde amnesia and the neuropsychology of memory. In L. S. Cermak (Ed.), *Human memory and amnesia* (pp. 275-304). Hillsdale, NJ: Erlbaum.

APA CODE: 4.16   INDEX NUMBER: 07

Gelfand, H., & Bjork, R. A. (1985, November). On *the locus of retrieval inhibition in directed forgetting.* Paper presented at the meeting of the Psychonomic Society, Boston.

APA CODE: 4.16   INDEX NUMBER: 08

Wermont v. Parish, 248 F. Supp. 1234 (E.D. Va. 1963).

APA CODE: Appendix D   INDEX NUMBER: 01

Adler, J. (1994, January 10). Kids growing up scared. *Newsweek, 73,* 43-49.

APA CODE: 4.16   INDEX NUMBER: 02

Trujillo, C. M. (1986). A comparative evaluation of classroom interactions between professors and minority and non-minority college students. *American Educational Research Journal, 23,* 629–642.

APA CODE: 5.18   INDEX NUMBER: 01

Janoff-Bulman, R. (1979). Characterological versus behavioral self-blame: Inquiries into depression and rape. *Journal of Personality and Social Psychology, 37,* 1798-1809.

Correct as is.   APA CODE: 5.18   INDEX NUMBER: 02

Klatzky, R. L. (1980). *Human Memory: Structures and Processes* (Second Edition). San Francisco: Freeman.

APA CODE: 4.16   INDEX NUMBER: 05

Yamamoto, T., Yayama, N., & Kawamura, Y. (1981). Central processing of taste perception. In Y. Katsuki, R. Norgren, and M. Sato, Editors, *Brain mechanisms of sensation* (pp. 197-208). New York: Wiley.

APA CODE: 4.16   INDEX NUMBER: 06

Squire, L. R., & Cohen, N. J. (1982). "Remote memory, retrograde amnesia and the neuropsychology of memory" (pp. 275-304). In Cermak, L. S. (Ed.), *Human memory and amnesia*. Hillsdale, NJ: Erlbaum.

APA CODE: 4.16   INDEX NUMBER: 07

Gelfand, H., & Bjork, R. A. *On the locus of retrieval inhibition in directed forgetting.* Paper presented at the meeting of the Psychonomic Society, Boston, November, 1985.

APA CODE: 4.16   INDEX NUMBER: 08

Wermont v. Parish, 248 Federal Supplement 1234 (E.D. Virginia 1963).

APA CODE: Appendix D   INDEX NUMBER: 01

Adler, J. (1994,). Kids growing up scared. *Newsweek,* , pp. 43-49.

APA CODE: 4.16   INDEX NUMBER: 02

Trujillo, C. M. (1986). A comparative evaluation of classroom interactions between professors and minority and non-minority college students. *American Educational Research Journal, 23,* 629-642.

APA CODE: 5.18   INDEX NUMBER: 01

Janoff-Bulman, R. (1979). Characterological versus behavioral self-blame: Inquiries into depression and rape. *Journal of Personality and Social Psychology, 37,* 1798-1809.

APA CODE: 5.18   INDEX NUMBER: 02

References

Hamburg, D. A., Elliott, G. R., & Parron, D. L. (Eds.). (1982). *Health and behavior: Frontiers of research in the biobehavioral sciences.* Washington, DC: National Academy Press.

APA CODE: 5.18   INDEX NUMBER: 03

Integrative Exercise: Reference List and Typing the Parts of a Manuscript

References

Frankenhaeuser, M. (1975). Sympathetic-adrenomedullary activity, behavior and the psychosocial environment. In P. H. Venables & M. J. Christie (Eds.), *Research in psychophysiology* (pp. 71-94). New York: Wiley.

Frankenhaeuser, M., & Jarpe, G. (1963). Psychophysiological changes during infusions of adrenaline in various doses. *Psychopharmacologia, 4,* 424-432.

Frankenhaeuser, M., Jarpe, G., & Mattell, G. (1961). Effects of intravenous infusions of adrenaline and noradrenaline on certain physiological and psychological functions. *Acta Physiologica Scandinavica, 51,* 175-186.

Krantz, D. S., Schaeffer, M. A., Davia, J. E., Dembroski, T. M., MacDougall, J. M., & Shaffer, R. T. (1981). Extent of atherosclerosis, Type A behavior, and cardiovascular response to social interaction. *Psychophysiology, 18,* 654-664.

APA CODES: 4.01–4.05, 5.18, Appendix D   INDEX NUMBER: 02

REFERENCES

Hamburg, D. A., Elliott, G. R., & Parron, D. L. (Eds.). (1982). *Health and behavior: Frontiers of research in the biobehavioral sciences.* Washington, DC: National Academy Press.

APA CODE: 5.18   INDEX NUMBER: 03

Integrative Exercise: Reference List and Typing the Parts of a Manuscript

References

Frankenhaeuser, M. (1975). *Sympathetic-adrenomedullary activity, behavior and the psychosocial environment* (pp. 71-94). In Venables, P. H., & Christie, M. J. (Eds.), Research in Psychophysiology. New York: Wiley.

Frankenhaeuser, M. and Jarpe, G. (1963). Psychophysiological changes during infusions of adrenaline in various doses. *Psychopharmacologia, 4,* 424-432.

Frankenhaeuser, M., Jarpe, G. & Mattell, G. (1961). "Effects of Intravenous Infusions of Adrenaline and Noradrenaline on Certain Physiological and Psychological Functions." *Acta physiologica Scandinavica, 51,* pp. 175-186.

Krantz, D. S., Schaeffer, M. A., Davia, J. E., Dembroski, T. M., MacDougall, J. M., & Shaffer, R. T. (1981). "Extent of atherosclerosis, Type A behavior, and cardiovascular response to social interaction." *Psychophysiology, 18,* 654-664.

APA CODES: 4.01–4.05, 5.18, Appendix D   INDEX NUMBER: 02

Term Paper Practice Test

The practice test, formatted like the familiarization test, is designed to (a) assess your level of mastery after completing the exercises, (b) help you to decide whether you need to study particular topics in the *Publication Manual* in more depth, (c) help you to decide whether to go on to the review exercises, and (d) help you to decide whether to take a mastery test. There are two answer sheets at the end of the test, one with blanks for you to write in your answers and the other containing the correct answers. Beside each blank you will find the APA code that corresponds to the number of the section in the *Publication Manual* where you can find the answer to that question. Score your test yourself. If you score low (i.e., 80% or lower) on the practice test, you should do the review exercises at the end of the term paper unit. If you score above 80%, you may want to take a mastery test, which your instructor will supply.

TERM PAPER PRACTICE TEST

1. Which characteristic of a manuscript helps readers grasp the paper's outline and the relative importance of its parts?

   a. voice
   b. verb tense
   c. hypotheses
   d. headings
   e. all of the above

2. A manuscript title should

   a. use abbreviations wherever possible.
   b. contain at least 30 words.
   c. be fully explanatory when standing alone.
   d. begin with the words *A Study of*.

3. The orderly presentation of ideas will become disorderly if the writer

   a. cues the reader to the subordination of ideas with punctuation.
   b. misplaces words.
   c. abandons familiar syntax.
   d. does all of the above.
   e. does b and c.

4. Which of the following phrases is redundant?

   a. a total of 68 respondents
   b. has been previously found
   c. in close proximity
   d. all of the above
   e. none of the above

5. Colloquial expressions such as *write-up*, approximations of quantity such as *quite a large part*, and informal or imprecise use of verbs such as *the client felt that*

   a. reduce word precision and clarity.
   b. add warmth to dull scientific prose.
   c. have a place even in serious scientific writing.
   d. can be used to enhance communication.
   e. are more acceptable in written as compared with oral communication.

6. Edit the following for verb tense:

Wrightsman and Deaux (1981) would demonstrate the same effect.

a. leave as is

b. Wrightsman and Deaux (1981) demonstrated the same effect.

c. Wrightsman and Deaux (1981) demonstrate the same effect.

d. The same effect was demonstrated by Wrightsman and Deaux (1981).

7. Which of the following sentences is grammatically correct?

a. Name the participant whom you found scored above the median.

b. The rats that completed the test successfully were rewarded.

c. We had nothing to do with them being the winners.

d. None of the above is correct.

8. Edit the following for the placement of modifiers:

To manipulate ego-involvement, the respondents were given different average scores for their norm group.

a. leave as is

b. To manipulate ego-involvement, we gave the respondents different average scores for their norm group.

c. Manipulating ego-involvement, the respondents were given different average scores for their norm group.

d. The respondents were given different average scores for their norm group to manipulate ego-involvement.

9. Edit the following for the use of subordinate conjunctions:

The more skilled athletes chose individual sports, while the less skilled athletes chose team sports.

a. leave as is

b. The more skilled athletes chose individual sports, and, at the same time, the less skilled athletes chose team sports.

c. The more skilled athletes chose individual sports, whereas the less skilled athletes chose team sports.

d. Both a and b are correct.

10. Which of the following should be used in scientific writing?

    a. rhyming
    b. poetic expressions
    c. sexist language
    d. none of the above

11. Edit the following for the use of nonsexist language:

    The data in Table 2 are the proportion of male participants who selected the competitive action over the cooperative one on each trial and, similarly, the proportion of female participants who were willing to act aggressively on each trial.

    a. leave as is

    b. The data in Table 2 are the proportion of male and female participants who selected the competitive action over the cooperative one on each trial.

    c. The data in Table 2 are the proportion of male participants who selected the competitive action over the cooperative one on each trial and the proportion of female participants who were willing to act aggressively on each trial.

    d. The data in Table 2 are the proportion of males who selected the competitive action over the cooperative one on each trial and, similarly, the proportion of females who were willing to act in typically male fashion (aggressively) on each trial.

12. In choosing nouns referring to ethnic groups, one should use

    a. the most acceptable current terms.
    b. the standard terms of the media.
    c. anthropological terms.
    d. none of the above.

13. Edit the following for punctuation:

The confederate always sat to the experimenter's immediate left and the experimenter began the discussion by asking the confederate to evaluate the therapist's degree of empathy.

a. leave as is

b. The confederate always sat to the experimenter's immediate left; and the experimenter began the discussion by asking the confederate to evaluate the therapist's degree of empathy.

c. The confederate always sat to the experimenter's immediate left, the experimenter began the discussion by asking the confederate to evaluate the therapist's degree of empathy.

d. The confederate always sat to the experimenter's immediate left. The experimenter began the discussion by asking the confederate to evaluate the therapist's degree of empathy.

14. Use a semicolon
a. to set off a nonessential or nonrestrictive clause.
b. to separate two independent clauses that are not joined by a conjunction.
c. in references between place of publication and publisher.
d. to do all of the above.

15. Edit the following for the punctuation of ratios:

Moving from the lowest subordinate level of the organization to the highest executive level, the ratios of men to women were 1.2 to 1, 2 to 1, 6 to 1, and 14 to 1, respectively.

a. leave as is

b. Moving from the lowest subordinate level of the organization to the highest executive level, the ratios of men/women were 1.2/1, 2/1, 6/1, and 14/1, respectively.

c. Moving from the lowest subordinate level of the organization to the highest executive level, the ratios of men:women were 1.2:1, 2:1, 6:1, and 14:1, respectively.

d. Moving from the lowest subordinate level of the organization to the highest executive level, the ratios of men-women were 1.2-1, 2-1, 6-1, and 14-1, respectively.

16. Edit the following for punctuation:

    The children: none of whom had previously heard the story: listened as a master storyteller told the story.

    a. leave as is

    b. The children; none of whom had previously heard the story; listened as a master storyteller told the story.

    c. The children ... none of whom had previously heard the story ... listened as a master storyteller told the story.

    d. The children--none of whom had previously heard the story--listened as a master storyteller told the story.

17. Edit the following for punctuation of the anchor points on a rating scale:

    The respondents ranked each of the 30 characteristics on a scale ranging from "most like my mother" (1) to "most like my father" (5).

    a. leave as is

    b. The respondents ranked each of the 30 characteristics on a scale ranging from MOST LIKE MY MOTHER (1) to MOST LIKE MY FATHER (5).

    c. The respondents ranked each of the 30 characteristics on a scale ranging from: most like my mother (1) to: most like my father (5).

    d. The respondents ranked each of the 30 characteristics on a scale ranging from *most like my mother* (1) to *most like my father* (5).

18. Punctuation is used incorrectly in which example?

    a. The results were significant (see Figure 5).

    b. Smith and Jones, 1970, reported results similar to those of Walker (1976).

    c. The GSR of rodents is unreliable (Adams & Baker, 1957).

    d. "When sea turtles were studied, the effect was not seen" (p. 276).

19. Edit the following for quotation from a source:

    According to Hebb (1949), the phase sequence for a familiar event is well organized, so "it runs its course promptly, leaving the field for less well-established sequences" [p. 229].

    a. leave as is

    b. According to Hebb (1949), the phase sequence for a familiar event is well organized, so "it runs its course promptly, leaving the field for less well-established sequences," p. 229.

    c. According to Hebb (1949), the phase sequence for a familiar event is well organized, so "it runs its course promptly, leaving the field for less well-established sequences (p. 229)".

    d. According to Hebb (1949), the phase sequence for a familiar event is well organized, so "it runs its course promptly, leaving the field for less well-established sequences" (p. 229).

20. Which of the following examples needs a hyphen?
    a. a posteriori test
    b. Type II error
    c. 12th grade students
    d. unbiased

21. Which of the examples contains incorrect capitalization?

    a. During Trial 5, Group B performed at criterion.

    b. Column 5, Row 3

    c. The animals ate Purina Lab Chow after tail-pinch administration.

    d. In his book, *History of Psychology*, the author describes Small's first use of the white rat.

22. Which word in the following sentence should be italicized?

    Snails were much faster when allowed to bathe ad lib in the acetylcholine solution.

    a. acetylcholine
    b. ad lib
    c. snails
    d. bathe
    e. none of the above

23. Which Latin abbreviation is used incorrectly in the following example?

When management styles were compared (authoritarian vs. participatory), it was found that authoritarian managers, i.e., those who did not solicit or act on input from subordinates, did not do well in smaller organizations (e.g., corporations with fewer than 100 employees).

a. vs.
b. i.e.
c. e.g.
d. all of the above
e. none of the above

24. Edit the following two levels of headings:

Amphibian Phobias

Fear of Forest Newts

a. leave as is

b.

Amphibian Phobias

Fear of Forest Newts

c.

Amphibian Phobias

FEAR OF FOREST NEWTS

d.

Amphibian Phobias

Fear of Forest Newts

25. Edit the following for the presentation of a series:

The participants were divided into three groups: (1) Experts, who had completed at least four courses in computer programming; (2) Intermediates, who had completed one course in computer programming and (3) Novices, who had no experience in computer programming.

a. leave as is

b. The participants were divided into three groups: (a) Experts, who had completed at least four courses in computer programming, (b) Intermediates, who had completed one course in computer programming, and (c) Novices, who had no experience in computer programming.

c. The participants were divided into three groups: a) experts, who had completed at least four courses in computer programming, b) intermediates, who had completed one course in computer programming, and c) novices, who had no experience in computer programming.

d. The participants were divided into three groups: (a) experts, who had completed at least four courses in computer programming; (b) intermediates, who had completed one course in computer programming; and (c) novices, who had no experience in computer programming.

26. Direct quotations
   a. must follow the wording, spelling, and interior punctuation of the original source even if incorrect. Errors in the original source are indicated with [*sic*].
   b. must follow the wording and interior punctuation of the original source, but any spelling errors should be corrected.
   c. should follow the original source but minor changes in wording, spelling, and interior punctuation are permissible.
   d. None of the above is correct.

27. Edit the following for the citation of a reference in text:

Women are often motivated by a fear of success rather than by a need to achieve because of the negative consequences they experience when they succeed in areas that are traditionally male dominated (Horner, 1970).

a. leave as is

b. Women are often motivated by a fear of success rather than by a need to achieve because of the negative consequences they experience when they succeed in areas that are traditionally male dominated--Horner, 1970.

c. Women are often motivated by a fear of success rather than by a need to achieve because of the negative consequences they experience when they succeed in areas that are traditionally male dominated (Horner: 1970).

d. Women are often motivated by a fear of success rather than by a need to achieve because of the negative consequences they experience when they succeed in areas that are traditionally male dominated: Horner (1970).

28. Edit the following for the citation of a reference in text:

Another possibility is that differences in IQ scores between Blacks and Whites are mediated by differences in family size. Family size has been shown to be related to IQ score (Zajonc, Markus, & Markus, 1979).

a. leave as is

b. Another possibility is that differences in IQ scores between Blacks and Whites are mediated by differences in family size. Family size has been shown to be related to IQ score (Zajonc & Markus & Markus, 1979).

c. Another possibility is that differences in IQ scores between Blacks and Whites are mediated by differences in family size. Family size has been shown to be related to IQ score (Zajonc, Markus, Markus, 1979).

d. Another possibility is that differences in IQ scores between Blacks and Whites are mediated by differences in family size. Family size has been shown to be related to IQ score (Zajonc, Markus, and Markus, 1979).

29. Choose the correct citation:

a. (Dorrow & O'Neal, 1979; Mullaney, 1978; Tapers, 1981)

b. (Zalichin, 1978, 1979, 1980)

c. Mullaney, 1978; Dorrow & O'Neal, 1979; Tapers, 1981)

d. b and c

e. a and b

30. Edit the folllowing for the citation of references in text:

> Biofeedback training may not affect alpha-wave regulation (Lynch, Paskewitz, & Orne, 1974, Miller, 1974, Plotkin & Cohen, 1976).

a. leave as is

b. Biofeedback training may not affect alpha-wave regulation (Lynch, Paskewitz, & Orne, 1974; Miller, 1974; Plotkin & Cohen, 1976).

c. Biofeedback training may not affect alpha-wave regulation (Lynch/Paskewitz/Orne: 1974; Miller: 1974; Plotkin/Cohen: 1976).

d. Biofeedback training may not affect alpha-wave regulation (Lynch, Paskewitz, & Orne, 1974: Miller, 1974: Plotkin & Cohen, 1976).

31. When citing a direct quotation from a source, be sure to give

a. the authors' names.
b. the year of publication.
c. the page number.
d. all of the above.
e. the authors' names and the year of publication.

32. If no author is given for a source, put the source in the correct order in the reference list by

a. moving the title to the author position and alphabetizing by the first significant word of the title.
b. beginning the entry with the word *Anonymous* and alphabetizing as if this were the author's name.
c. moving the journal title or publishing house to the author position and alphabetizing by the first significant word of the name.
d. Do none of the above.

33. In a reference list, when ordering several works by the same first author,

a. place single-author entries before multiple-author entries.
b. do not repeat the first author's name after the first entry.
c. you may order them alphabetically by the name of the journal.
d. All of the above are correct.

34. Edit the following for the application of APA reference style:

Lovaas, O. I., Schaeffer, B., and Simmons, J. Q. (1965). Building social behavior in autistic children by use of electric shock. *Journal of Experimental Research in Personality*, 1, 99-109.

a. leave as is

b. Lovaas, O. I., Schaeffer, B., & Simmons, J. Q. (1965). Building social behavior in autistic children by use of electric shock. *Journal of Experimental Research in Personality*, 1, 99-109.

c. Lovaas, O. I., et al. (1965). Building social behavior in autistic children by use of electric shock. *Journal of Experimental Research in Personality*, 1, 99-109.

d. Lovaas, O. I., Schaeffer, B., Simmons, J. Q. (1965). Building social behavior in autistic children by use of electric shock. *Journal of Experimental Research in Personality*, 1, 99-109.

35. Edit the following for the application of APA reference style:

Roveé-Collier, C. (1984). "The ontogeny of learning and memory in human infancy." In Kail, R., and Spear, N. E. (Eds.), *Comparative perspectives on the development of memory* (pp. 103-134). Hillsdale, NJ: Erlbaum.

a. leave as is

b. Roveé-Collier, C. (1984). *The ontogeny of learning and memory in human infancy*. In R. Kail & N. E. Spear (Eds.), "Comparative Perspectives on the Development of Memory (pp. 103-134)." Hillsdale, NJ: Erlbaum.

c. Roveé-Collier, C. (1984). The ontogeny of learning and memory in human infancy. In R. Kail & N. E. Spear (Eds.), *Comparative perspectives on the development of memory* (pp. 103-134). Hillsdale, NJ: Erlbaum.

d. Roveé-Collier, C. (1984). The ontogeny of learning and memory in human infancy. In Kail, R., & Spear, N. E. (Editors), *Comparative perspectives on the development of memory* (pp. 103-134). Hillsdale, NJ: Erlbaum.

36. Which kind of spacing should not be used anywhere in a manuscript?
a. single-spacing
b. double double-spacing
c. triple-spacing
d. all of the above

37. The right margin should

    a. have divided words to achieve an even margin.
    b. not have divided words and may be uneven.
    c. have a 1-in. (2.54-cm) space rather than a 2-in. (5.08-cm) space.
    d. have divided or undivided words to achieve a clean line.

38. When correcting typing errors,

    a. retype the page if any errors are made.
    b. correct neatly using correction paper, fluid, or tape to cover the error and then type the correction.
    c. correct the word-processing file and make a clean printout.
    d. type an insert on a slip and attach it to the page with one staple.
    e. b and c.

39. In most cases, space once after all of the following punctuation marks except

    a. periods in a reference citation.
    b. periods ending a sentence.
    c. internal periods in abbreviations.
    d. colons.

40. Edit the following for typing a title page:

    COOPERATIVE AND COMPETITIVE PROCESSES IN ACADEMIC WORK

    Harold Gelfand and Charles J. Walker

    St. Bonaventure University

    a. leave as is

    b.

    Cooperative and Competitive Processes in Academic Work

    Harold Gelfand and Charles J. Walker

    St. Bonaventure University

    c.

    Cooperative and Competitive Processes in Academic Work

    Harold Gelfand & Charles J. Walker

    St. Bonaventure University

    d.

    Cooperative and Competitive Processes in Academic Work

    Harold Gelfand   Charles J. Walker

    St. Bonaventure University   St. Bonaventure University

41. Edit the following for the application of APA electronic reference style:

> VandenBos, G., Knapp, S., & Doe, J. (2001). Role of reference elements in the selection of resources by psychology undergraduates. *Journal of Bibliographic Research, 5,* 117-123 (electronic version).

a. VandenBos, G., Knapp, S., & Doe, J. (2001). Role of reference elements in the selection of resources by psychology undergraduates [Electronic version]. *Journal of Bibliographic Research, 5,* 117-123.

b. VandenBos, G., Knapp, S., & Doe, J. (2001). Role of reference elements in the selection of resources by psychology undergraduates (electronic version). *Journal of Bibliographic Research, 5,* 117-123.

c. VandenBos, G., Knapp, S., & Doe, J. (2001). Role of reference elements in the selection of resources by psychology undergraduates [electronic version]. *Journal of Bibliographic Research, 5,* 117-123.

d. VandenBos, G., Knapp, S., & Doe, J. (2001). Role of reference elements in the selection of resources by psychology undergraduates. *Journal of Bibliographic Research, 5,* 117-123 [Electronic version].

42. Edit the following for the application of APA electronic reference style:

> VandenBos, G., Knapp, S., & Doe, J. (2001, October 13). Role of reference elements in the selection of resources by psychology undergraduates. *Journal of Bibliographic Research, 5,* 117-123. Retrieved online from http://jbr.org/articles.html

a. leave as is

b. VandenBos, G., Knapp, S., & Doe, J. (2001). Role of reference elements in the selection of resources by psychology undergraduates. *Journal of Bibliographic Research, 5,* 117-123. Retrieved October 13, 2001, from http://jbr.org/articles.html

c. VandenBos, G., Knapp, S., & Doe, J. (2001, October 31). Role of reference elements in the selection of resources by psychology undergraduates [Retrieved from http://jbr.org/articles.html]. *Journal of Bibliographic Research, 5,* 117-123.

d. VandenBos, G., Knapp, S., & Doe, J. (2001). Role of reference elements in the selection of resources by psychology undergraduates. *Journal of Bibliographic Research, 5,* 117-123 [retrieved October 13, 2001, from http://jbr.org/articles.html].

TERM PAPER PRACTICE TEST
ANSWER SHEET AND FEEDBACK REPORT

Student Name _____ **Date** _____

Question Number	Answer	APA Codes	Question Number	Answer	APA Codes
1	_____	1.03–1.05	22	_____	3.19
2	_____	1.06–1.08	23	_____	3.20–3.29
3	_____	2.01–2.02	24	_____	3.30–3.33
4	_____	2.03–2.04	25	_____	3.30–3.33
5	_____	2.03–2.04	26	_____	3.34–3.41
6	_____	2.06–2.07	27	_____	3.94–3.103
7	_____	2.08–2.11	28	_____	3.94–3.103
8	_____	2.08–2.11	29	_____	3.94–3.103
9	_____	2.08–2.11	30	_____	3.94–3.103
10	_____	2.13–2.17	31	_____	3.94–3.103
11	_____	2.13–2.17	32	_____	4.01–4.04
12	_____	2.13–2.17	33	_____	4.01–4.04
13	_____	3.01–3.09	34	_____	4.01–4.04
14	_____	3.01–3.09	35	_____	4.01–4.04
15	_____	3.01–3.09	36	_____	5.01–5.08
16	_____	3.01–3.09	37	_____	5.01–5.08
17	_____	3.01–3.09	38	_____	5.01–5.08
18	_____	3.01–3.09	39	_____	5.09–5.13
19	_____	3.01–3.09	40	_____	5.15–5.16
20	_____	3.10–3.11	41	_____	4.16
21	_____	3.12–3.18	42	_____	4.16

NUMBER CORRECT _____

TERM PAPER PRACTICE TEST
ANSWER KEY

Question Number	Answer	APA Codes
1	d	1.03–1.05
2	c	1.06–1.08
3	e	2.01–2.02
4	d	2.03–2.04
5	a	2.03–2.04
6	b	2.06–2.07
7	b	2.08–2.11
8	b	2.08–2.11
9	c	2.08–2.11
10	d	2.13–2.17
11	b	2.13–2.17
12	a	2.13–2.17
13	d	3.01–3.09
14	b	3.01–3.09
15	c	3.01–3.09
16	d	3.01–3.09
17	d	3.01–3.09
18	b	3.01–3.09
19	d	3.01–3.09
20	c	3.10–3.11
21	b	3.12–3.18

Question Number	Answer	APA Codes
22	e	3.19
23	b	3.20–3.29
24	d	3.30–3.33
25	d	3.30–3.33
26	a	3.34–3.41
27	a	3.94–3.103
28	a	3.94–3.103
29	e	3.94–3.103
30	b	3.94–3.103
31	d	3.94–3.103
32	a	4.01–4.04
33	a	4.01–4.04
34	b	4.01–4.04
35	c	4.01–4.04
36	d	5.01–5.08
37	b	5.01–5.08
38	e	5.01–5.08
39	c	5.09–5.13
40	b	5.15–5.16
41	a	4.16
42	b	4.16

Term Paper Review Exercises

NOTES:

Review Exercise: Parts of a Manuscript and Typing the Parts of a Manuscript

Computer Simulations

1

Running head: COMMUNICATION MODELS OF ORGANIZATIONS

Computer Simulations of Communication Processes in Vertically
Structured Organizations

Hy R. Kichal, Art E. Fishel, and Mack N. Tosh

Upsy Downsy National University

Millie Tarry and B. Yuri Craddick

Department of Political Chemistry

Unelectoral College

APA CODES: 1.06–1.15, 5.15–5.22   INDEX NUMBER: 02

Term Paper Review Exercises

Review exercises are all in the integrative format and cover the same style rules as the learning exercises and integrative exercises. Complete the review exercises as you did the integrative exercises, by reading the exercises on the right-hand page, writing your corrections on that page, and comparing your corrections to the correct version of the exercise on the left. Review exercises are designed to give you additional practice, to help you review style points you have already studied, and to further prepare you to take a mastery test.

Review Exercise: Parts of a Manuscript and Typing the Parts of a Manuscript

Communication Models

Computer simulations of communication processes in vertically

structured organizations

Hy R. Kichal, Art E. Fishel, Mack N. Tosh

Upsy Downsy National University

Millie Tarry & B. Yuri Craddick

Department of Political Chemistry, Unelectoral College

Communication Models of Organizations

APA CODES: 1.06–1.15, 5.15–5.22   INDEX NUMBER: 02

Review Exercise: Grammar

Past research suggests that teaching methods influence student learning. The most common teaching method, the traditional lecture, has been shown to be ineffective when compared with most other teaching methods. However, Cross and Angelo (1988) predicted that student learning will increase if lecturers are given the opportunity to assess student learning before, during, or after lecturing. To test their hypothesis Magoo (1990) divided instructors into two groups: One group used classroom assessment techniques and the other used no assessment techniques. All of the instructors taught Economics 101 for one semester. To measure learning, students took the same final examination, and to obtain comparable instructor evaluations, students rated their instructor on the same evaluation instrument. As Magoo predicted, students scored higher on the final when their instructors used assessment techniques. Also, students rated instructors who used classroom assessment techniques higher on effectiveness, enthusiasm, and competence than instructors who did not use assessment techniques.

These results suggest that assessing student learning while lecturing improves student learning as well as instructor evaluations. Although Magoo's data are suggestive, they are neither definitive nor conclusive. Peer review and long-term student achievement are criterion measures that must be examined before one can conclude that classroom assessment positively affects teaching and learning.

APA CODES: 2.06–2.12   INDEX NUMBER: 02

Review Exercise: Grammar

Past research suggests that teaching methods influence student learning. The most common teaching method, the traditional lecture, has shown to be ineffective when compared with most other methods. However, Cross and Angelo (1988) predicted that student learning will increase if lecturers are given the opportunity to assess student learning before, during, or after lecturing. To test their hypothesis, Magoo (1990) had instructors divided into two groups: One group used classroom assessment techniques and the other used no assessment techniques. All of the instructors taught Economics 101 for one semester. To measure learning, students took the same final examination, and to obtain comparable instructor evaluations, students rated his or her instructor on the same evaluation instrument. As predicted, students scored higher on the final when they were taught by instructors using assessment techniques. Also, students rated instructors which used classroom assessment techniques higher on effectiveness, enthusiasm, and competence than instructors whom did not use assessment techniques.

These results suggest that assessing student learning while lecturing improves both student learning as well as instructor evaluations. While Magoo's data is suggestive, it is neither definitive or conclusive. Peer review and long-term student achievement is criteria measures that must be examined before it can be concluded that positively classroom assessment affects teaching and learning.

APA CODES: 2.06–2.12   INDEX NUMBER: 02

Review Exercise: Guidelines to Reduce Bias in Language

In a heterogeneous community, a therapist may serve clients from a variety of religious and ethnic backgrounds, many different from the therapist's own. The client brings a set of values or expectations to therapy, based on experiences in the family and community. Of course, the therapist also has a set of values related to his or her own cultural and educational background that, no matter how different from that of the client, the therapist must be careful not to impose on him or her. Even if the therapist is sensitive to the cultural differences, the therapist has to avoid letting biases or expectations--about what the values and expectations that are influencing the client should be or actually are--interfere with his or her ability to understand and serve the client. Each therapist may require special exposure to, and training about, the cultural values and experiences of the clients she or he serves in order to maximize therapeutic effectiveness.

It may even be that clients would be better served if they were matched with therapists who share their religious and ethnic heritages. Black clients might fare better with Black therapists, Asian clients might fare better with Asian therapists, Hispanic clients might fare better with Hispanic therapists, and even White Catholics might fare better with White Catholic therapists. (Such matches might be impossible for some groups who do not yet have trained therapists among their members.) It is also possible that a therapist who is too much like his or her client will lose objectivity or that a client who is too much like his or her therapist will not engage in the therapeutic relationship fully. We conducted this investigation to determine whether such compatibility between therapist and client would affect therapeutic success as indicated by a variety of short- and long-term measures of success.

APA CODES: 2.13–2.17   INDEX NUMBER: 02

Review Exercise: Guidelines to Reduce Bias in Language

In a heterogeneous community, a therapist may serve clients from a variety of religious, ethnic backgrounds, many different from his own. The client brings her own set of values or expectations to therapy, based on her own experiences in her family and community. Of course, the therapist also has a set of values related to his own cultural and educational background that, no matter how superior to that of his client, he must be careful not to impose on her. Even if the therapist is sensitive to the cultural differences, the therapist has to avoid letting his own biases or expectations-- about what the values and expectations that are influencing his client should be or actually are--interfere with his ability to understand and serve his client. Each therapist may require special exposure to, and training about, the cultural values and experiences of the clients he serves in order to maximize his therapeutic effectiveness.

It may even be that clients would be better served if they were matched with therapists who share their religious and ethnic heritages. Negro clients might fare better with Negro therapists; Oriental clients might fare better with Oriental therapists; Hispanic clients might fare better with Hispanic therapists; and even Caucasian catholics might fare better with Caucasian catholic therapists. (Such matches might be impossible for some backwards groups whose members are not bright enough to receive training as therapists yet.) It is also possible that a therapist who is too much like his client will lose his objectivity or that a client who is too much like her therapist will not engage in the therapeutic relationship fully. We conducted this investigation to determine whether such compatibility between therapist and client would affect therapeutic success as indicated by a variety of short- and long-term measures of success.

APA CODES: 2.13–2.17   INDEX NUMBER: 02

Review Exercise: Punctuation and General Typing Instructions

Cardiovascular disease is subject to a number of risk factors. Some of the risk factors -- family history of heart disease, age, and gender -- are genetic or cannot be modified but are important to identify for the purpose of monitoring cardiac functioning. Other risk factors -- cholesterol levels, cigarette smoking, and hypertension -- can be modified and therefore pose opportunities for the prevention of coronary disease or heart attacks. Cholesterol levels can be reduced through dietary modifications; cigarette smoking requires an obvious behavioral change; and hypertension, although often treated pharmacologically, can also be treated behaviorally. Given the potential side effects of antihypertension drugs and the frequent failures to take medications (perhaps due to the absence of overt symptoms), behavioral treatments are an attractive alternative or supplement to medical treatments. Hypertension can be reduced through dietary changes (resulting in weight reduction and diminished salt intake), increased exercise, and improvement in stress-coping skills. More direct effects on blood pressure are achieved through biofeedback and relaxation training.

APA CODES: 3.01–3.09, 5.11   INDEX NUMBER: 02

Review Exercise: Spelling and Hyphenation

Forgiveness of blasphemy was explored in a 2 x 2 between-subjects factorial design. Low-dogmatic individuals were compared with high-dogmatic individuals in their willingness to forgive a person who published a blasphemous essay or a highly revealing, kiss-and-tell essay. Blood pressure readings were taken before and after the forgiveness ratings. Planned comparisons were reported rather than the results of a two-way analysis of variance. Individuals who were high dogmatic were significantly less forgiving than low-dogmatic individuals, as determined by planned *t* tests. Blood pressure was highest in the lowest forgiveness condition.

APA CODES: 3.10–3.11   INDEX NUMBER: 02

Review Exercise: Punctuation and General Typing Instructions

Cardiovascular disease is subject to a number of risk factors. Some of the risk factors: family history of heart disease, age, gender, are genetic or cannot be modified, but are important to identify for the purpose of monitoring cardiac functioning, and other risk factors: cholesterol levels, cigarette smoking, hypertension, can be modified, and therefore pose opportunities for the prevention of coronary disease or heart attacks. Cholesterol levels can be reduced through dietary modifications, cigarette smoking requires an obvious behavioral change, and hypertension (although often treated pharmacologically) can also be treated behaviorally. Given the potential side effects of antihypertension drugs and the frequent failures to take medications (Perhaps due to the absence of overt symptoms.), behavioral treatments are an attractive alternative or supplement to medical treatments. Hypertension can be reduced through dietary changes (resulting in weight reduction, and diminished salt intake), increased exercise and improvement in stress-coping skills. More direct effects on blood pressure are achieved through biofeedback, and relaxation training.

APA CODES: 3.01–3.09, 5.11   INDEX NUMBER: 02

Review Exercise: Spelling and Hyphenation

Forgivness of blasfemy was explored in a 2 x 2 between-subjects factorial design. Low dogmatic individuals were compared with high dogmatic individuals in their willingness to forgive a person who published a blasfemous essay or a highly-revealing, kiss and tell essay. Blood-pressure readings were taken before-and-after the forgiveness-ratings. Planned compairsons were reported rather than the results of a two way analysis-of-variance. Individuals who were high-dogmatic were significantly less forgiving than low dogmatic individauls, as determined by planned t-tests. Blood-pressure was highest in the lowest-forgiveness condition.

APA CODES: 3.10–3.11   INDEX NUMBER: 02

Review Exercise: Capitalization and General Typing Instructions

Not all explanations of spider phobia assume that classical conditioning of irrational fear occurred at some point in the life of a patient (e.g., neo-Freudian theories). In fact, some theories of learning contend that there are biological constraints that favor the acquisition of some phobias over others (e.g., the biological preparedness theories of Garcia & Koelling, 1966, or Maser & Seligman, 1977).

APA CODES: 3.12–3.18, 5.09   INDEX NUMBER: 02

Review Exercise: Italics

Grope et al. (1927) reported in *Phrenology Today* that the reliability of temple reading can be increased (from a split-half index of .28 to .47) by coating the head of clients in beeswax. However, they emphasized, one must first shave the client's head.

APA CODE: 3.19   INDEX NUMBER: 02

Review Exercise: Abbreviations

Within the continental United States, since 1966 the rate of LSD consumption has decreased. In contrast, intravenously administered drugs such as cocaine have increased in consumption. Cocaine consumption might have increased because of the immediacy and desirability of the effects it produces (i.e., its users quickly feel euphoric). Milligrams of such drugs can produce radical shifts in mood. Needles as short as 1 in. (2.54 cm) can easily reach large veins (e.g., 0.20 cm or 0.30 cm) and thus produce rapid, pervasive effects. After an injection, the scores of users on the Minnesota Multiphasic Personality Inventory change, as do their reaction times (RTs) and short-term memory (STM) ability. Changes in RTs and STM ability last for relatively long durations.

APA CODES: 3.20–3.29   INDEX NUMBER: 02

Review Exercise: Capitalization and General Typing Instructions

Not all explanations of Spider Phobia assume that classical conditioning of irrational fear occurred at some point in the life of a patient (e.g., Neo-Freudian theories). in fact, some theories of learning contend that there are biological constraints that favor the acquisition of some phobias over others (e.g., the Biological Preparedness theories of Garcia & Koelling, 1966, or Maser & Seligman, 1977).

APA CODES: 3.12–3.18, 5.09   INDEX NUMBER: 02

Review Exercise: Italics

Grope *et al.* (1927) reported in Phrenology Today that the reliability of temple reading can be increased (from a *split-half index* of .28 to .47) by coating the head of clients in *beeswax*. However, they emphasized, one must first *shave* the client's head.

APA CODE: 3.19   INDEX NUMBER: 02

Review Exercise: Abbreviations

Within the continental U.S., since 1966 the rate of L.S.D. consumption has decreased. In contrast, intravenously administered drugs such as cocaine have increased in consumption. Cocaine consumption might have increased because of the immediacy and desirability of the effects it produces (that is, its users quickly feel euphoric). Mg's of such drugs can produce radical shifts in mood. Needles as short as 1 in (2.54 cms) can easily reach large veins (for example, 0.20 cm or 0.30 cm) and thus produce rapid, pervasive effects. After an injection, the scores of users on the MMPI change, as do their RT's and STM ability. Changes in RTs and STM ability last for relatively long durations.

APA CODES: 3.20–3.29   INDEX NUMBER: 02

Review Exercise: Headings and Series and General Typing Instructions

A History of Psychology

Early Laboratories

Harvard Laboratories

James's basement. Because Harvard University would not allow live animals on campus, William James converted the basement of his home into an animal laboratory. Edward Lee Thorndike did some of his first research on chickens in James's basement.

APA CODES: 3.30–3.33, 5.10, 5.12   INDEX NUMBER: 02

Review Exercise: Quotations and General Typing Instructions

According to Kurtz (1988), near death experiences (NDEs) have reasonable physiological explanations: "We know that when the body is badly injured the heart stops and cerebral anoxia occurs.... At first there may be a sense of well being, probably the result of the brain's endorphin response to extreme trauma" (p. 15).

APA CODES: 3.34–3.41, 5.13   INDEX NUMBER: 02

Review Exercise: Headings and Series and General Typing Instructions

A HISTORY OF PSYCHOLOGY

Early Laboratories

Harvard Laboratories

James's Basement: Because Harvard University would not allow live animals on campus, William James converted the basement of his home into an animal laboratory. Edward Lee Thorndike did some of his first research on chickens in James's basement.

APA CODES: 3.30–3.33, 5.10, 5.12   INDEX NUMBER: 02

Review Exercise: Quotations and General Typing Instructions

According to Kurtz (1988, p. 15), near death experiences (NDEs) have reasonable physiological explanations:

> We know that when the body is badly injured the heart stops and cerebral anoxia occurs... At first there may be a sense of well being, probably the result of the brain's endorphin response to extreme trauma.

APA CODES: 3.34–3.41, 5.13   INDEX NUMBER: 02

Review Exercise: Reference Citations in Text

Release from proactive inhibition (Wickens, 1970, 1972) and the tip-of-the-tongue phenomenon (Brown & McNeill, 1966) suggest that memory encodings are multidimensional. Although Craik and Lockhart (1972) proposed a levels-of-processing model that emphasized the nature of encoding operations, subsequent research (Craik & Tulving, 1975; Fisher & Craik, 1977; Moscovitch & Craik, 1976) indicated the central role of retrieval in memory performance. According to encoding specificity theory (Tulving & Osler, 1968; Tulving & Thomson, 1973), it is the match between encoding and retrieval operations that dictates memory performance. Tulving and Osler found that weak retrieval cues were superior to strong ones as long as the weak cues were also presented at the time of encoding. Research on environmental context (e.g., Smith, Glenberg, & Bjork, 1978) and internal states (e.g., Bower, 1981; Eich, 1980) indicates not only that external contexts become part of the encodings of information but also that a match between encoding and retrieval environments is crucial for maximizing memory performance.

APA CODES: 3.94–3.103   INDEX NUMBER: 02

Review Exercise: Reference Citations in Text

Release from proactive inhibition (Wickens, 1970; Wickens, 1972) and the tip-of-the-tongue phenomenon (Brown & McNeill, 1966) suggest that memory encodings are multidimensional. Although Craik & Lockhart (Craik & Lockhart, 1972) proposed a levels-of-processing model that emphasized the nature of encoding operations, subsequent research (Craik, & Tulving, 1975; Moscovitch & Craik, 1976; Fisher & Craik, 1977) indicated the central role of retrieval in memory performance. According to encoding specificity theory (Tulving and Osler, 1968; Tulving and Thomson, 1973), it is the match between encoding and retrieval operations that dictates memory performance. Tulving and Osler (1968) found that weak retrieval cues were superior to strong ones as long as the weak cues were also presented at the time of encoding. Research on environmental context (e.g., Smith, Glenberg & Bjork, 1978) and internal states (e.g., Bower: 1981; Eich: 1980) indicates not only that external contexts become part of the encodings of information but also that a match between encoding and retrieval environments is crucial for maximizing memory performance.

APA CODES: 3.94–3.103   INDEX NUMBER: 02

Review Exercise: Reference List and Typing the Parts of a Manuscript

References

Bjork, E. L., & Bjork, R. A. (1987). On the adaptive aspects of retrieval failure in autobiographical memory. In M. M. Gruneberg, P. E. Morris, & R. N. Sykes (Eds.), *Practical aspects of memory: Current research and issues: Vol. 1. Memory in everyday life* (pp. 283-288). London: Wiley.

Bjork, R. A. (1978). The updating of human memory. In G. H. Bower (Ed.), *Psychology of learning and motivation* (Vol. 12, pp. 235-259). San Diego, CA: Academic Press.

Bjork, R. A. (in press). Retrieval inhibition as an adaptive mechanism in human memory. In H. L. Roediger & F. I. M. Craik (Eds.), *Varieties of memory and consciousness: Essays in honour of Endel Tulving*. Hillsdale, NJ: Erlbaum.

Bjork, R. A., & Geiselman, R. E. (1978). Constituent processes in the differentiation of items in memory. *Journal of Experimental Psychology: Human Learning and Memory, 4,* 347-361.

Geiselman, R. E., MacKinnon, D. P., Fishman, D. L., Jaenicke, C., Larner, B., Schoenberg, S., & Swartz, S. (1983). Mechanisms of hypnotic and nonhypnotic forgetting. *Journal of Experimental Psychology: Learning, Memory, and Cognition, 9,* 626-635.

Gelfand, H., & Bjork, R. A. (1985, November). *On the locus of retrieval inhibition in directed forgetting.* Paper presented at the meeting of the Psychonomic Society, Boston.

Loomis, K. H., & Davis, C. A. (2001). Reading comprehension, editorial style, and memory. *Journal of Experimental Psychology: Human Learning and Memory, 27,* 468-475. Retrieved July 14, 2001, from http://jep.org/articles.html

- *Note to students:* You also should have changed the order of the references because they were not alphabetized correctly.

APA CODES: 4.01–4.05, 4.16, 5.18, Appendix D   INDEX NUMBER: 02

Review Exercise: Reference List and Typing the Parts of a Manuscript

References

Bjork, R. A., and Geiselman, R. E. (1978). Constituent processes in the differentiation of items in memory. *Journal of Experimental Psychology: Human Learning and Memory,* 4, 347-361.

Bjork, R. A. Retrieval Inhibition as an Adaptive Mechanism in Human Memory. In H. L. Roediger, & F. I. M. Craik, (Eds.), *Varieties of memory and consciousness: Essays in honour of Endel Tulving* (in press). Hillsdale, NJ: Erlbaum.

Bjork, R. A. (1978). *The updating of human memory* (pp. 235-259). In G. H. Bower, Editor, Psychology of Learning and Motivation, Vol. 12. San Diego, CA: Academic Press.

Bjork, E. L., & Bjork, R. A. (1987, pp. 283-288) "On the adaptive aspects of retrieval failure in autobiographical memory." In M. M. Gruneberg, P. E. Morris, and R. N. Sykes (Eds.), *Practical aspects of memory: Current research and issues: Vol. 1. Memory in everyday life.* London: Wiley.

Geiselman, R. E., MacKinnon, D. P., Fishman, D. L., Jaenicke, C., Larner, B., Schoenberg, S., & Swartz, S. (1983). Mechanisms of Hypnotic and Nonhypnotic Forgetting. *Journal of Experimental Psychology: Learning, Memory, and Cognition,* 9, 626-635.

Gelfand, H., & Bjork, R. A. (November, 1985). "On the locus of retrieval inhibition in directed forgetting." Paper presented at the meeting of the Psychonomic Society, Boston.

Loomis, K. H., & Davis, C. A. (2001, July 14). Reading comprehension, editorial style, and memory [Retrieved from http://jep.org/articles.html]. *Journal of Experimental Psychology: Human Learning and Memory, 27,* 468-475.

APA CODES: 4.01–4.05, 4.16, 5.18, Appendix D   INDEX NUMBER: 02

Term Paper Mastery Tests

The *Instructor's Resource Guide* contains four mastery tests for each unit (term paper and research report). Your instructor will decide whether to give you one or more mastery tests as a means to evaluate your knowledge of APA style and your readiness to prepare writing assignments. These tests are similar in structure and content to the familiarization and practice tests but contain different questions. Your instructor will provide you with the mastery tests and may or may not grade them; a grade is useful only for demonstrating that you have mastered APA style (90% correct is the standard for mastery unless your instructor announces otherwise).

Like the familiarization and practice tests, the mastery tests contain 40 multiple-choice questions, along with the APA codes indicating where in the *Publication Manual* you can find the answers. However, you may not use the *Publication Manual* as you take the tests. Your instructor will give you either a grade or feedback about the areas in which you need to work.

CHAPTER 4

Research Report Unit

4

The purpose of this unit is to provide you with the chance to learn and apply the APA style rules that will be most useful when you write research reports. Because this unit contains style requirements that are more advanced or more technical than the exercises in the term paper unit, you should do the latter unit first. This unit, like the term paper unit, is divided into four components: the familiarization test, learning exercises and integrative exercises, the practice test, and review exercises. Begin by taking the familiarization test, which will help you to identify what you do and do not know about APA style with regard to writing research reports.

Research Report Familiarization Test

By taking this test and reviewing your responses, you will be able to determine whether you are familiar with the APA style requirements related to writing research reports. The test contains 40 multiple-choice items. There are two answer sheets at the end of the test, one with blanks for you to write in your answers and the other containing the answers. APA codes are next to each answer blank; they correspond to the sections in the *Publication Manual* containing the relevant style rule. Read each test item and the possible responses, and write the letter of the response on the blank answer sheet. You may consult the *Publication Manual* at any time. It may be useful to mark questions that you found to be difficult. After taking this test, check your answers against the answer key and score your test, but count only those questions that you answered without using the *Publication Manual*. If the total number of incorrect answers plus looked-up answers is 8 or more (20% or more incorrect), we advise you to complete all of the learning exercises. If you did well on the test (i.e., at least 36 of 40 correct), you may want to skip the learning exercises and take the practice test that follows these exercises or take a mastery test.

RESEARCH REPORT FAMILIARIZATION TEST

1. In contrast to empirical or theoretical articles, review articles

   a. define and clarify a problem.
   b. summarize previous investigations.
   c. identify relations, contradictions, or inconsistencies in the literature.
   d. suggest steps for future research.
   e. do all of the above.

2. Which of the following must identify the specific variables investigated and the relation between them?

    a. the first sentence of the introduction section
    b. the conclusion of the Discussion section
    c. the title of the report
    d. the first table that is cited

3. An abstract for a research report should be about

    a. 100 to 120 words.
    b. 75 to 100 words.
    c. 100 to 150 words.
    d. 150 to 200 words.

4. Conventionality and expediency dictate that the Method section should be written

    a. as a unified whole.
    b. in subsections.
    c. without reference notes.
    d. Answers a and c are correct.
    e. None of the above is correct.

5. When describing human participants, you should state

    a. the number of participants who did not complete the experiment.
    b. the total number of participants.
    c. the number of participants assigned to each experimental condition.
    d. all of the above.
    e. b and c of the above.

6. In reporting tests of significance,

    a. give the exact value of the statistic (F or t value).
    b. state the relevant degrees of freedom.
    c. indicate the probability level.
    d. describe the direction of an effect.
    e. do all of the above.

7. If your study is simple and your Discussion section is brief and straightforward, you can

    a. discuss the flaws of the study at length.
    b. spend most of your time discussing the next study you plan to do.
    c. combine the Results and Discussion sections.
    d. discuss the negative findings, listing all of the possible causes.
    e. do all of the above.

8. On the basis of verb tense, in which part of a report is the following text segment likely to appear?

> College students judge time differently than do college faculty. Faculty are more accurate in judging the amount of time required to do academic tasks.

   a. Method
   b. a review of the literature in an introduction
   c. a conclusion in a Discussion
   d. Results

9. Approximations of quantity such as *a major portion of*, colloquial expressions such as *write-up*, or informal verb use such as *it was her feeling that*

   a. reduce word precision and clarity.
   b. add warmth to dull scientific prose.
   c. have a place in serious scientific writing.
   d. can be used to enhance communication.
   e. are more acceptable in written than in oral communication.

10. In table headings and figure captions,

   a. capitalize only the first word and proper nouns.
   b. capitalize all major words.
   c. do not capitalize any words.
   d. capitalization will depend on the message you wish to convey.

11. Names of conditions or groups in an experiment should

   a. be capitalized.
   b. not be capitalized.
   c. not be capitalized unless followed by numerals or letters.
   d. be designated by a letter.

12. Use italics for

   a. trigonometric terms.
   b. introduction of key terms and labels.
   c. Greek letters.
   d. all of the above.

13. Edit the following by selecting the correct arrangement of headings:

Experiment 1

Method

Stimulus Materials

 Animal sounds.

a. leave as is

b.

Experiment 1

Method

Stimulus Materials

 Animal sounds.

c.

EXPERIMENT 1

Method

Stimulus Materials

 Animal sounds.

d.

EXPERIMENT 1

Method

Stimulus Materials

Animal sounds.

14. Use numerical figures to express

 a. any number that begins a sentence.
 b. common fractions.
 c. numbers that immediately precede a unit of measurement.
 d. none of the above.

15. Edit the following for the expression of numbers:

    Respondents in each of the age groups were asked to describe what they had eaten for dinner two and four weeks previously.

    a. leave as is

    b. Respondents in each of the age groups were asked to describe what they had eaten for dinner 2 and 4 weeks previously.

16. Edit the following for the expression of numbers:

    Eighty nurses volunteered to keep a daily record of their stress levels.

    a. leave as is

    b. 80 nurses volunteered to keep a daily record of their stress levels.

    c. Eighty (80) nurses volunteered to keep a daily record of their stress levels.

17. Words should be used to express numbers
    a. whenever numbers are greater than 20 but less than 200.
    b. from zero to nine, not representing a precise measurement and not grouped for comparison with numbers 10 and above.
    c. always, except when cardinal numbers have satisfied the requirements of ratio measurement and are grouped for comparison with themselves.
    d. as seldom as possible.

18. Edit the following for the expression of ordinal numbers:

    The critical stimuli were placed in the second and 10th positions in each block of trials.

    a. leave as is

    b. The critical stimuli were placed in the 2nd and 10th positions in each block of trials.

    c. The critical stimuli were placed in the second and tenth positions in each block of trials.

19. Edit the following for the expression of decimal fractions:

    The containers were made of transparent plastic and weighed .6 kg.

    a. leave as is

    b. The containers were made of transparent plastic and weighed 0.6 kg.

    c. The containers were made of transparent plastic and weighed 6×10^{-1} kg.

    d. The containers were made of transparent plastic and weighed 60×10^{-2} kg.

20. Edit the following for the expression of numbers:

    When the payoff for finding an effective treatment is so high, it is important to minimize Type 2 errors.

    a. leave as is

    b. When the payoff for finding an effective treatment is so high, it is important to minimize Type II errors.

    c. When the payoff for finding an effective treatment is so high, it is important to minimize Type Two errors.

21. Use commas between groups of three digits in figures of 1,000 or more except when expressing

    a. page numbers.
    b. serial numbers.
    c. degrees of freedom.
    d. all of the above.

22. Edit the following for the correct use of metric measurement:

    Conductance and inductance were measured in siemens (S) and henrys (H), respectively.

    a. leave as is
    b. The measurements do not conform to the International System of Units.
    c. Measurements should not be expressed in metric units in social or behavioral science journals.
    d. Inductance should be measured in newtons per meter, not in henrys.

23. When you present statistics, cite the reference

    a. for less common statistics.
    b. for statistics used in a controversial way.
    c. when a statistic itself is the focus of an article.
    d. for all of the above.
    e. for any statistics and all uses of a statistic.

24. Edit the following for the expression of formulas:

   The participants were told their mean reaction times (M = total reaction time/ number of trials) after each block of trials.

   a. leave as is

   b. The participants were told their mean reaction times ($M = \Sigma RT/n$ trials) after each block of trials.

   c. The participants were told their mean reaction times [$M = (RT_1 + RT_2 + RT_3 \ldots + RT_n)n_T$] after each block of trials.

   d. The participants were told their mean reaction times after each block of trials.

25. Which of the following is the correct way to present a statistic in text?

   a. F = 2.62(22), $p<.01$

   b. $t(22) = 2.62$, $p <. 01$

   c. t = 2.62(22), $p <. 01$

   d. none of the above

26. Edit the following for the presentation of statistics:

   The children were divided into two groups on the basis of which hand they used to hold the pen. The mean scores on the orientation task for the two groups were 34 and 142.

   a. leave as is

   b. The children were divided into two groups on the basis of which hand they used to hold the pen. The mean scores on the orientation task for the left-handed and right-handed groups were 34 and 142, respectively.

   c. The children were divied into two groups on the basis of which hand they used to hold the pen. The mean scores on the orientation task for the left-handed and right-handed groups were 34 and 142.

   d. The children were divied into two groups on the basis of which hand they used to hold the pen. The mean scores on the orientation task for the two groups were 34 and 142, respectively.

27. Edit the following for the presentation of statistical symbols:

> Respondents who received feedback after each response hit more targets (mean = 74.4, standard deviation = 9.7) than did those who received feedback after each block of 24 responses (mean = 44.7, standard deviation = 2.3), t(30) = 3.42, p < .01.

   a. leave as is

   b. Respondents who received feedback after each response hit more targets (M = 74.4, SD = 9.7) than did those who received feedback after each block of 24 responses (M = 44.7, SD = 2.3), t(30) = 3.42, p < .01.

   c. Respondents who received feedback after each response hit more targets ($\bar{X}$ = 74.4, SD = 9.7) than did those who received feedback after each block of 24 responses ($\bar{X}$ = 44.7, SD = 2.3), t(30) = 3.42, p < .01.

   d. Respondents who received feedback after each response hit more targets (*M* = 74.4, *SD* = 9.7) than did those who received feedback after each block of 24 responses (*M* = 44.7, *SD* = 2.3), *t*(30) = 3.42, *p* < .01.

28. Before constructing a table, you should consider that

   a. rounded-off values display patterns more clearly than precise values.
   b. readers can compare numbers down a column more easily than across rows.
   c. data from a 2 × 2 design should be put in a table rather than in the text.
   d. adding space between columns or rows can make a table easier to read.
   e. all of the above except c.

29. A good table

   a. is intelligible without reference to the text.
   b. does not need to be discussed in the text.
   c. duplicates information in the text.
   d. does a and b of the above.

30. Tables should be numbered in the order

   a. that puts the longest table first.
   b. in which they are first mentioned in the text.
   c. that seems most logical to the author.
   d. that seems most logical to an editor.

31. The left-hand column of a table (the stub) has a heading (the stubhead) that usually lists the

   a. elements in that column.
   b. dependent variables.
   c. independent variables.
   d. data.
   e. a and c.

32. When more than one level of significance is reported in a table,

    a. each level is represented by a single asterisk.
    b. one asterisk is used for the lowest level.
    c. another asterisk is added for each level of significance.
    d. b and c are correct.

33. Tables, including titles and headings, should be

    a. triple-spaced.
    b. double-spaced.
    c. single-spaced.
    d. any of the above.

34. The word *figure* refers to

    a. halftones.
    b. graphs and charts.
    c. illustrations.
    d. all of the above.

35. What kind of graph (a type of figure) is useful to show a continuous change across time?

    a. bar
    b. circle
    c. line
    d. pie
    e. scatter

36. From the following examples, select the correct way to refer to a figure in text:

    a. see the figure above

    b. see the figure on page 14

    c. see Figure 2

    d. see Figure 2 above on page 14

37. Which of the following is the correct ordering of manuscript subsections?

    a. title page, introduction, abstract
    b. References, appendixes, author identification notes
    c. Method, Discussion, Results
    d. figures, figure captions, tables
    e. Discussion, footnotes, References

38. If the title of your manuscript is *Effects of Deviant Revealing on the Mood States of the Chronically Happy*, and your running head is REVELATION AND HAPPINESS, what short title should you use?

    a. Effects of Deviant

    b. Revelation and Happiness

    c. Deviant Revealing and the Mood of the Chronically Happy

    d. Chronic Revealing

39. Edit the following for typing the title page:

EFFECTIVENESS OF TRAINING METHODS FOR MASTERING APA STYLE

Harold Gelfand and Charles J. Walker

St. Bonaventure University

a. leave as is

b.

Effectiveness of Training Methods for Mastering APA Style

Harold Gelfand and Charles J. Walker

St. Bonaventure University

c.

Effectiveness of Training Methods for Mastering APA Style

Harold Gelfand & Charles J. Walker

St. Bonaventure University

d.

Effectiveness of Training Methods for Mastering APA Style

Harold Gelfand   Charles J. Walker

St. Bonaventure University   St. Bonaventure University

40. The abstract should

a. appear on the same page above the title and introduction.
b. be single-spaced and set with larger margins.
c. begin on page 2.
d. be no longer than 3% of the text.

RESEARCH REPORT FAMILIARIZATION TEST
ANSWER SHEET AND FEEDBACK REPORT

Student Name _____ **Date** _____

Question Number	Answer	APA Codes	Question Number	Answer	APA Codes
1	_____	1.01–1.05	21	_____	3.42–3.49
2	_____	1.06–1.07	22	_____	3.50–3.52
3	_____	1.06–1.07	23	_____	3.53–3.59
4	_____	1.08–1.09	24	_____	3.53–3.59
5	_____	1.08–1.09	25	_____	3.53–3.59
6	_____	1.10–1.13	26	_____	3.53–3.59
7	_____	1.10–1.13	27	_____	3.53–3.59
8	_____	2.01–2.02	28	_____	3.62–3.72
9	_____	2.03–2.05	29	_____	3.62–3.72
10	_____	3.12–3.18	30	_____	3.62–3.72
11	_____	3.12–3.18	31	_____	3.62–3.72
12	_____	3.19	32	_____	3.62–3.72
13	_____	3.30–3.33	33	_____	3.74
14	_____	3.42–3.49	34	_____	3.75–3.81
15	_____	3.42–3.49	35	_____	3.75–3.81
16	_____	3.42–3.49	36	_____	3.83–3.84
17	_____	3.42–3.49	37	_____	5.01–5.08
18	_____	3.42–3.49	38	_____	5.01–5.08
19	_____	3.42–3.49	39	_____	5.15–5.25
20	_____	3.42–3.49	40	_____	5.15–5.25

NUMBER CORRECT _____

RESEARCH REPORT FAMILIARIZATION TEST
ANSWER KEY

Question Number	Answer	APA Codes	Question Number	Answer	APA Codes
1	e	1.01–1.05	21	d	3.42–3.49
2	c	1.06–1.07	22	a	3.50–3.52
3	a	1.06–1.07	23	d	3.53–3.59
4	b	1.08–1.09	24	d	3.53–3.59
5	d	1.08–1.09	25	d	3.53–3.59
6	e	1.10–1.13	26	b	3.53–3.59
7	c	1.10–1.13	27	d	3.53–3.59
8	c	2.01–2.02	28	e	3.62–3.72
9	a	2.03–2.05	29	a	3.62–3.72
10	a	3.12–3.18	30	b	3.62–3.72
11	c	3.12–3.18	31	e	3.62–3.72
12	b	3.19	32	d	3.62–3.72
13	b	3.30–3.33	33	b	3.74
14	c	3.42–3.49	34	d	3.75–3.81
15	b	3.42–3.49	35	c	3.75–3.81
16	a	3.42–3.49	36	c	3.83–3.84
17	b	3.42–3.49	37	b	5.01–5.08
18	b	3.42–3.49	38	a	5.01–5.08
19	b	3.42–3.49	39	b	5.15–5.25
20	b	3.42–3.49	40	c	5.15–5.25

Research Report Learning Exercises and Integrative Exercises

The learning exercises and integrative exercises appear in two versions: draft (incorrect) and feedback (correct). The feedback and draft versions appear on the left- and right-hand pages, respectively. There are APA codes under each section title as well as below each exercise; these codes correspond to the relevant parts of the *Publication Manual*.

There are two types of exercises: learning (short) and integrative. Learning exercises are brief excerpts of text that address one or two components of APA style (e.g., metrication, numbers). The components that are being targeted (i.e., in need of correction) are shaded. Read the text of the draft version on the right-hand page and decide whether the shaded text is correct or incorrect. Write corrections on the workbook page directly above the errors. You may consult the *Publication Manual* at any time. Check your answers against the feedback version on the left-hand page to see whether your answer is correct. The feedback version will state "correct as is," or the correctly edited material will be shaded.

Integrative exercises consist of a paragraph or page of text that you are to edit. The components in need of correction are not shaded, but the errors in each integrative exercise are all related to the style rules applied in the preceding group of learning exercises. Read the text carefully and edit the text, marking corrections directly on the draft version. The corrections on the feedback page are shaded. Integrative exercises appear at the end of each group of learning exercises.

Capitalization and General Typing Instructions
APA Codes: 3.12–3.18, 5.09

NOTES:

On the 3rd day of Experiment 2, the children read chapter 6 of their sex education text. Then there was a discussion about sexual transmission of disease.

APA CODE: 3.15   INDEX NUMBER: 01

As can be seen in Table 9 and Figure 2, clients who were misinformed about sex as children were also more likely to believe in sexual myths as adults.

APA CODE: 3.15   INDEX NUMBER: 02

The control groups were counterbalanced across both Condition A and Condition B.

APA CODE: 3.17   INDEX NUMBER: 01

Participants in the tobacco-chewing therapy condition and the no-therapy control condition then received two wads of chewing tobacco.

APA CODE: 3.17   INDEX NUMBER: 02

Sarcastic sentences were remembered better than nonsarcastic sentences; however, there was no Sarcasm x Sex x Self-Esteem interaction effect.

APA CODE: 3.18   INDEX NUMBER: 01

An analysis of variance showed that the between-subjects variable was significant.

APA CODE: 3.18   INDEX NUMBER: 02

Capitalization and General Typing Instructions
APA Codes: 3.12–3.18, 5.09

These exercises cover capitalization of (a) nouns followed by numerals or letters; (b) titles of tests; (c) names of conditions or groups in an experiment; and (d) names of factors, variables, and effects (see the *Publication Manual*, sections 3.12–3.18 and 5.09). Mark corrections directly on the right-hand page, and compare your responses with the correct answers on the left-hand page. When you are finished with this section, go on to the next section in which you need practice.

On the 3rd day of experiment 2, the children read chapter 6 of their sex education text. Then there was a discussion about sexual transmission of disease.

APA CODE: 3.15   INDEX NUMBER: 01

As can be seen in table 9 and figure 2, clients who were misinformed about sex as children were also more likely to believe in sexual myths as adults.

APA CODE: 3.15   INDEX NUMBER: 02

The Control Groups were counterbalanced across both condition A and condition B.

APA CODE: 3.17   INDEX NUMBER: 01

Participants in the tobacco-chewing therapy condition and the No-Therapy control condition then received two wads of chewing tobacco.

APA CODE: 3.17   INDEX NUMBER: 02

Sarcastic sentences were remembered better than nonsarcastic sentences; however, there was no sarcasm X sex X self-esteem interaction effect.

APA CODE: 3.18   INDEX NUMBER: 01

An analysis of variance showed that the between-subjects factor was significant.

APA CODE: 3.18   INDEX NUMBER: 02

Integrative Exercise: Capitalization and General Typing Instructions

On Trial 26 of Experiment 9, Boreal owls (*Aegolius funereus*) were reintroduced as pets in the huts of those elderly Algonquins who were assigned to the therapy condition. Feather dusters were given to the control groups to assess placebo effects. After 2 weeks of contact with the feathered stimuli, all participants received the Peck Reality Orientation Scale.

APA CODES: 3.12–3.18, 5.09   INDEX NUMBER: 01

Abbreviations
APA Codes: 3.20–3.29

NOTES:

The Minnesota Multiphasic Personality Inventory (MMPI) was administered to respondents of different handedness, 26 left-handed and 62 right-handed.

APA CODES: 3.20 & 3.23   INDEX NUMBER: 01

Three kinds of odor tests were presented to college students: odor recognition (OR), odor discrimination (OD), and odor matching (OM). Tests were administered in either the OD-OR-OM or OM-OR-OD sequence.

APA CODES: 3.20 & 3.21   INDEX NUMBER: 02

Low doses of LSD seemed to have no effect on the ESP of pygmy chimpanzees.

Correct as is.   APA CODE: 3.22   INDEX NUMBER: 01

Integrative Exercise: Capitalization and General Typing Instructions

On trial 26 of Experiment 9, boreal owls (*Aegolius funereus*) were reintroduced as pets in the huts of those elderly Algonquins who were assigned to the Therapy Condition. Feather dusters were given to the control groups to assess Placebo Effects. After 2 Weeks of contact with the feathered stimuli, all participants received the Peck reality orientation scale.

APA CODES: 3.12–3.18, 5.09   INDEX NUMBER: 01

Abbreviations
APA Codes: 3.20–3.29

These exercises cover the use of abbreviations, explaining abbreviations, abbreviations accepted as words, abbreviations used in APA journals, Latin abbreviations, abbreviations of units of measurement and statistics, use of periods with abbreviations, plurals of abbreviations, and abbreviations beginning a sentence (see the *Publication Manual*, sections 3.20–3.29). Mark corrections directly on the right-hand page, and compare your responses with the correct answers on the left-hand page. When you are finished with this section, go on to the next section in which you need practice.

The MMPI was administered to respondents of different handedness, 26 LH and 62 RH.

APA CODES: 3.20 & 3.23   INDEX NUMBER: 01

Three kinds of odor tests were presented to college students: odor recognition (OR), odor discrimination (OD), and odor matching (OM). Tests were administered in either the OD-OR-OM or OM-OR-OD sequence.

APA CODES: 3.20 & 3.21   INDEX NUMBER: 02

Low doses of LSD seemed to have no effect on the ESP of pygmy chimpanzees.

APA CODE: 3.22   INDEX NUMBER: 01

Before the children were given the test weights to judge, 20 children were asked to move 10 blocks that weighed 1 kg each and 20 children were asked to move 10 blocks that weighed 4 kg each.

APA CODE: 3.28   INDEX NUMBER: 01

Pounds of weight loss was recorded as the dependent variable, and hours spent with the phobic object was the independent variable.

APA CODE: 3.29   INDEX NUMBER: 01

Integrative Exercise: Abbreviations

IQ tests were administered to 480 subjects who recently completed BA, MA, or PhD degrees in psychology. All of the students were then given the General Aptitude in Psychology (GAP) test. As predicted, no effects of education were observed with either the IQ or the GAP test as the criterion measure (i.e., BA, MA, and PhD students were not different in either intelligence or aptitude).

APA CODES: 3.20–3.29   INDEX NUMBER: 01

Before the children were given the test weights to judge, 20 children were asked to move 10 blocks that weighed 1 kg each and 20 children were asked to move 10 blocks that weighed 4 kgs each.

APA CODE: 3.28   INDEX NUMBER: 01

lbs of weight loss was recorded as the dependent variable, and hours spent with the phobic object was the independent variable.

APA CODE: 3.29   INDEX NUMBER: 01

Integrative Exercise: Abbreviations

Intelligence quotient tests were administered to 480 Ss who recently completed BA, MA, or Ph.D. degrees in psychology. All of the students were then given the General Aptitude in Psychology (GAP) test. As predicted, no effects of education were observed with either the IQ or the General Aptitude in Psychology (GAP) test as the criterion measure (i.e., BA, MA, and Ph.D. students were not different in either intelligence or aptitude).

APA CODES: 3.20–3.29   INDEX NUMBER: 01

NOTES:

Method

Participants

Materials

Procedure

Results

Discussion

References

APA CODE: 3.30   INDEX NUMBER: 01

Method

Participants

Procedure

    Early experience.

    Experimental training.

    Testing.

Results

Discussion

References

APA CODES: 3.30–3.32   INDEX NUMBER: 02

Headings and Series and General Typing Instructions
APA Codes: 3.30–3.33, 5.10, 5.12

These exercises cover organizing a manuscript with headings, levels of headings, selecting the levels of headings, and seriation (see the *Publication Manual*, sections 3.30–3.33, 5.10, and 5.12). Mark corrections directly on the right-hand page and compare your responses with the correct answers on the left-hand page. When you are finished with this section, go on to the next section in which you need practice.

Introduction

Method

Participants

Materials

Procedure

Results

Discussion

References

APA CODE: 3.30   INDEX NUMBER: 01

Method

Participants

Procedure

    Early experience.

    Experimental training.

    Testing.

Results

Discussion

References

APA CODES: 3.30–3.32   INDEX NUMBER: 02

Experiment 1

Method

Participants

Materials

    Client descriptions.

    Rating scales.

Procedure

    Assessment training.

    Client familiarization.

    Client evaluation.

Results

Discussion

Experiment 2

Method

Participants

Materials

Procedure

Results

Discussion

General Discussion

References

Correct as is.   APA CODES: 3.30–3.32 INDEX NUMBER: 03

Stimulus materials. the four episodes evaluated by the different groups were identical except for the descriptions of the client's history and the behavior that led to the client being brought to the therapist.

APA CODE: 3.31 INDEX NUMBER: 01

Experiment 1

Method

Participants

Materials

    Client descriptions.

    Rating scales.

Procedure

    Assessment training.

    Client familiarization.

    Client evaluation.

Results

Discussion

Experiment 2

Method

Participants

Materials

Procedure

Results

Discussion

General Discussion

References

APA CODES: 3.30–3.32   INDEX NUMBER: 03

Stimulus Materials. The four episodes evaluated by the different groups were identical except for the descriptions of the client's history and the behavior that led to the client being brought to the therapist.

APA CODE: 3.31   INDEX NUMBER: 01

Method

Subjects

    Captive animals. The subjects were 96 nocturnal mammals from a zoo in Canada and another 96 nocturnal mammals from a zoo in Australia.

APA CODE: 3.31   INDEX NUMBER: 02

Method

Subjects

Procedure

    Treatment.

    Immediate evaluation.

    Delayed evaluation.

Results

Discussion

References

APA CODES: 3.31–3.32   INDEX NUMBER: 03

Prior to being timed on the test puzzle, the respondents had one of five experiences with a similar puzzle: (a) watched an expert solve the puzzle, (b) watched a novice solve the puzzle, (c) solved the puzzle alone, (d) looked at the puzzle without working on it, and (e) had no experience.

APA CODE: 3.33   INDEX NUMBER: 01

Method

Subjects:

Captive Animals: The subjects were 96 nocturnal mammals from a zoo in Canada and another 96 nocturnal mammals from a zoo in Australia.

APA CODE: 3.31   INDEX NUMBER: 02

METHOD

Subjects

Procedure

Treatment

Immediate Evaluation

Delayed Evaluation

RESULTS

DISCUSSION

REFERENCES

APA CODES: 3.31–3.32   INDEX NUMBER: 03

Prior to being timed on the test puzzle, the respondents had one of five experiences with a similar puzzle: (1) watched an expert solve the puzzle, (2) watched a novice solve the puzzle, (3) solved the puzzle alone, (4) looked at the puzzle without working on it, and (5) had no experience.

APA CODE: 3.33   INDEX NUMBER: 01

All participants underwent the same sequence of events:

1. They completed a form anonymously that provided demographic information.

2. They filled out the Multiple Affect Adjective Check List (MAACL).

3. They completed the sex role inventory.

4. They observed the videotape appropriate for the condition to which the subject had been assigned.

5. They filled out the MAACL again.

Correct as is.   APA CODE: 3.33   INDEX NUMBER: 02

The adolescents were divided into 18 groups according to whether they selected a role model who was (a) Black, White, or Hispanic; (b) male or female; and (c) an athlete, entertainer, or scientist.

APA CODE: 3.33   INDEX NUMBER: 03

Method

Participants

APA CODE: 5.10   INDEX NUMBER: 01

All participants underwent the same sequence of events:

1. They completed a form anonymously that provided demographic information.

2. They filled out the Multiple Affect Adjective Check List (MAACL).

3. They completed the sex role inventory.

4. They observed the videotape appropriate for the condition to which the subject had been assigned.

5. They filled out the MAACL again.

APA CODE: 3.33   INDEX NUMBER: 02

The adolescents were divided into 18 groups according to whether they selected a role model who was (a) Black, White, or Hispanic, (b) male or female, and (c) an athlete, entertainer, or scientist.

APA CODE: 3.33   INDEX NUMBER: 03

METHOD

Participants

APA CODE: 5.10   INDEX NUMBER: 01

Experiment 2

In Experiment 1, the gender of another person was shown to affect a child's expectations of the behavior of that person. We conducted Experiment 2 for three purposes:

1. One goal was to test whether the gender-based expectations identified in Experiment 1 depend on the age of the other person.

2. If age of the object-person is a mediating factor, then a second purpose was to determine whether the expectations of the behavior of boys or girls change more with the age of the object-person.

3. Our final goal was to determine how the behavior of children toward another person changes as a function of the age of the other person, regardless of the gender of the other person.

Method

Respondents

The respondents were one hundred twenty 4-year-old boys and one hundred twenty 4-year-old girls attending nursery schools in the urban and suburban sections of a major city. None of the children who participated in Experiment 1 participated in Experiment 2. Informed consent for the child's participation was obtained from the parent or legal guardian of each child who participated.

Design

The experiment was a 2 x 2 x 4 between-subjects design. The sex of the respondent was a selected variable. The sex and age (8, 12, 20, and 60 years old) of the storyteller to whom each child was assigned was manipulated. Fifteen girls and 15 boys were randomly assigned to each of the eight (Sex x Age) storyteller conditions.

(*continued*)

EXPERIMENT 2

Introduction

In Experiment 1, the gender of another person was shown to affect a child's expectations of the behavior of that person. We conducted Experiment 2 for three purposes:

(1) One goal was to test whether the gender-based expectations identified in Experiment 1 depend on the age of the other person.

(2) If age of the object-person is a mediating factor, then a second purpose was to determine whether the expectations of the behavior of boys or girls change more with the age of the object-person.

(3) Our final goal was to determine how the behavior of children toward another person changes as a function of the age of the other person, regardless of the gender of the other person.

Method

Respondents: The respondents were one hundred twenty 4-year-old boys and one hundred twenty 4-year-old girls attending nursery schools in the urban and suburban sections of a major city. None of the children who participated in Experiment 1 participated in Experiment 2. Informed consent for the child's participation was obtained from the parent or legal guardian of each child who participated.

Design: The experiment was a 2 x 2 x 4 between-subjects design. The sex of the respondent was a selected variable. The sex and age (8, 12, 20, and 60 years old) of the storyteller to whom each child was assigned was manipulated. Fifteen girls and 15 boys were randomly assigned to each of the eight (Sex x Age) storyteller conditions.

(*continued*)

Procedure

Storytellers and storyteller training. The 20-year-old storytellers were the same two people who served as storytellers in Experiment 1. The 8- and 12-year-old storytellers were two girls and two boys who were recommended by their teachers and school librarian on the basis of their avid interest in reading and their skills in reading aloud. The 60-year-old storytellers were a man and a woman who served as literacy volunteers and volunteer readers in the children's program of the local public library. The storytellers were trained following the same procedures as were used in Experiment 1.

APA CODES: 3.30–3.33, 5.10, 5.12   INDEX NUMBER: 01

Numbers
APA Codes: 3.42–3.49

NOTES:

The inventory consists of 30 personal characteristics to be rated by the respondent.

APA CODE: 3.42   INDEX NUMBER: 01

In 9 of those studies, women scored higher; in 7, men scored higher; and in the other 12, no reliable differences between men and women were observed.

APA CODE: 3.42   INDEX NUMBER: 02

Procedure

Storytellers and Storyteller Training: The 20-year-old storytellers were the same two people who served as storytellers in Experiment 1. The 8- and 12-year-old storytellers were two girls and two boys who were recommended by their teachers and school librarian on the basis of their avid interest in reading and their skills in reading aloud. The 60-year-old storytellers were a man and a woman who served as literacy volunteers and volunteer readers in the children's program of the local public library. The storytellers were trained following the same procedures as were used in Experiment 1.

APA CODES: 3.30–3.33, 5.10, 5.12   INDEX NUMBER: 01

Numbers
APA Codes: 3.42–3.49

These exercises give you practice in using numbers expressed as numerals, numbers expressed in words, combining figures and words to express numbers, ordinal numbers, decimal fractions, arabic or roman numerals, commas in numbers, and plurals of numbers (see the *Publication Manual*, sections 3.42–3.49). Mark corrections directly on the right-hand page, and compare your responses with the correct answers on the left-hand page. When you are finished with this section, go on to the next section in which you need practice.

The inventory consists of thirty personal characteristics to be rated by the respondent.

APA CODE: 3.42   INDEX NUMBER: 01

In nine of those studies, women scored higher; in seven, men scored higher; and in the other 12, no reliable differences between men and women were observed.

APA CODE: 3.42   INDEX NUMBER: 02

Each child read four stories and answered 12 reading comprehension questions about each story.

APA CODE: 3.42   INDEX NUMBER: 03

Minority group characters were portrayed as responsible for the solution of a problem in only 6% of the episodes in which they appeared.

Correct as is.   APA CODE: 3.42   INDEX NUMBER: 04

The clients were returned to the clinic for assessment 1 week and 5 weeks after the last group therapy session.

Correct as is.   APA CODE: 3.42   INDEX NUMBER: 05

Because of mechanical failure, 7 participants did not complete the session, and their data were eliminated.

APA CODE: 3.42   INDEX NUMBER: 06

The greatest increase in responding was between Trial 2 and Trial 3.

APA CODE: 3.42   INDEX NUMBER: 07

The sketches presented to the different groups contained 2, 3, 4, 5, and 6 facial features, respectively.

APA CODE: 3.42   INDEX NUMBER: 08

Each set of letters could be arranged to form either of two words.

Correct as is.   APA CODE: 3.43   INDEX NUMBER: 01

A total of 53 clients volunteered. Forty were selected on the basis of clinical histories and treatment to date.

APA CODE: 3.43   INDEX NUMBER: 02

There were 16 pictures in each condition. Eight pictures were of familiar people, and 8 were of unfamiliar people.

Correct as is.   APA CODE: 3.43   INDEX NUMBER: 03

Each child read 4 stories and answered 12 reading comprehension questions about each story.

Minority group characters were portrayed as responsible for the solution of a problem in only 6% of the episodes in which they appeared.

The clients were returned to the clinic for assessment 1 week and 5 weeks after the last group therapy session.

Because of mechanical failure, seven participants did not complete the session, and their data were eliminated.

The greatest increase in responding was between Trial Two and Trial Three.

The sketches presented to the different groups contained two, three, four, five, and six facial features, respectively.

Each set of letters could be arranged to form either of two words.

A total of 53 clients volunteered. 40 were selected on the basis of clinical histories and treatment to date.

There were 16 pictures in each condition. Eight pictures were of familiar people, and 8 were of unfamiliar people.

In the conjunctive condition, the group could not go on to the next step until at least three fourths of the group members had mastered the previous step.

APA CODE: 3.43   INDEX NUMBER: 04

Each story was read to fifteen 5 -year-olds and fifteen 8 -year-olds.

APA CODE: 3.44   INDEX NUMBER: 01

The first block of trials was a practice set.

Correct as is.   APA CODE: 3.45   INDEX NUMBER: 01

The third graders and fifth graders were given a rest after the 20th trial in each block.

APA CODE: 3.45   INDEX NUMBER: 02

The mean number of absences by the 24 students was 3.7.

APA CODE: 3.46   INDEX NUMBER: 01

The greater the number of people who viewed the program together, the poorer was their memory for details (r) = - .63).

APA CODE: 3.46   INDEX NUMBER: 02

The procedure for Experiment 2 was identical to that used in Experiment 1, except that the child did not receive feedback after each trial.

APA CODE: 3.47   INDEX NUMBER: 01

The participants were shown real or fabricated newspaper stories that had appeared in either the 1950s, 1960s, or 1970s.

APA CODE: 3.49   INDEX NUMBER: 01

In the conjunctive condition, the group could not go on to the next step until at least 3/4 of the group members had mastered the previous step.

APA CODE: 3.43   INDEX NUMBER: 04

Each story was read to 15 5-year-olds and 15 8-year-olds.

APA CODE: 3.44   INDEX NUMBER: 01

The first block of trials was a practice set.

APA CODE: 3.45   INDEX NUMBER: 01

The 3rd graders and 5th graders were given a rest after the 20th trial in each block.

APA CODE: 3.45   INDEX NUMBER: 02

The mean number of absences by the 24 students was 3.6666667.

APA CODE: 3.46   INDEX NUMBER: 01

The greater the number of people who viewed the program together, the poorer was their memory for details ($r = -0.63$).

APA CODE: 3.46   INDEX NUMBER: 02

The procedure for Experiment II was identical to that used in Experiment I, except that the child did not receive feedback after each trial.

APA CODE: 3.47   INDEX NUMBER: 01

The participants were shown real or fabricated newspaper stories that had appeared in either the 1950's, 1960's, or 1970's.

APA CODE: 3.49   INDEX NUMBER: 01

Food supply was expected to affect aggression, but it was not clear what effect it would have on jumping behavior. Musical upbringing was expected to affect jumping behavior but not aggression, especially when food was abundant. No long-term effects of either variable were expected.

Method

Subjects

Ninety-six frogs were selected from the frog pool of the Calaveras County Jumping Academy. An expert judged their ages to be between 8 and 60 days since emerging from their tadpole state. Direct measurements indicated that the thickness of their rear-upper legs ranged from 0.65 cm to 4.85 cm.

Design

A 2 x 3 factorial design was used to manipulate the food supply (limited or abundant) and the musical environment (rock and roll, popular, or classical) of the frogs. Groups of 6 frogs, matched within 0.05 cm on thickness of rear-upper legs, were randomly assigned to the six conditions, resulting in the assignment of 16 frogs to each condition.

Apparatus

Seven identical enclosed, air-conditioned habitats were constructed, each containing a grassy area surrounding a pond. The pond contained pond water ranging in depth from 0.1 m to 2.7 m, pond mud at the bottom, numerous rocks and lily pads, and other vegetation found in the frogs' natural habitat.

(continued)

Food supply was expected to affect aggression, but it was not clear what effect it would have on jumping behavior. Musical upbringing was expected to affect jumping behavior but not aggression, especially when food was abundant. No long-term effects of either variable were expected.

Method

Subjects

96 frogs were selected from the frog pool of the Calaveras County Jumping Academy. An expert judged their ages to be between eight and 60 days since emerging from their tadpole state. Direct measurements indicated that the thickness of their rear-upper legs ranged from .65 cm to 4.85 cm.

Design

A 2 x 3 factorial design was used to manipulate the food supply (limited or abundant) and the musical environment (rock and roll, popular, or classical) of the frogs. Groups of six frogs, matched within 0.05 cm on thickness of rear-upper legs, were randomly assigned to the six conditions, resulting in the assignment of 16 frogs to each condition.

Apparatus

Seven identical enclosed, air-conditioned habitats were constructed, each containing a grassy area surrounding a pond. The pond contained pond water ranging in depth from .1 m to 2.7 m, pond mud at the bottom, numerous rocks and lily pads, and other vegetation found in the frogs' natural habitat.

(continued)

Procedure

The 16 frogs that were assigned to a particular condition were placed in one of the six identical habitats and kept there for a total of 8 weeks, except for individual testing (as described in the next paragraph), which was conducted in the seventh habitat. The frogs in the six experimental conditions received different treatments during Days 1-14. In the limited-supply habitats, 400 flies were introduced daily; in the abundant-supply habitats, 1,600 flies were introduced daily. In each habitat, music periods of 2 hr's duration alternated with quiet periods of 2 hr's duration. The music was piped in over loudspeakers. Eight selections, each lasting 0.25 hr, were chosen for the rock and roll, popular, and classical conditions. Appendix 1 contains the list of specific selections for each musical condition. For each condition, six different tape recordings of the eight selections in a different random order were made. Each of the six tapes was piped into the habitat during one of the six music periods each day.

Each frog was observed in its group habitat by three observers for 5 min on Day 14. The observers (who were blind to the experimental condition--they wore headphones over which bullfrog croakings were played to mask the musical condition) counted the number of aggressive acts, the number of jumps, and the length of the longest jump (the starting and landing spots were marked on a sketch of the habitat, and jump length was later converted to distance in meters using a blueprint of the habitat) by the frog being observed.

APA CODES: 3.42–3.49   INDEX NUMBER: 01

Procedure

The sixteen frogs that were assigned to a particular condition were placed in one of the 6 identical habitats and kept there for a total of 8 weeks, except for individual testing (as described in the next paragraph), which was conducted in the 7th habitat. The frogs in the six experimental conditions received different treatments during Days 1-14. In the limited-supply habitats, 400 flies were introduced daily; in the abundant-supply habitats, 1600 flies were introduced daily. In each habitat, music periods of two hr's duration alternated with quiet periods of two hr's duration. The music was piped in over loudspeakers. Eight selections, each lasting 0.25 hr, were chosen for the rock and roll, popular, and classical conditions. Appendix I contains the list of specific selections for each musical condition. For each condition, 6 different tape recordings of the eight selections in a different random order were made. Each of the 6 tapes was piped into the habitat during one of the six music periods each day.

Each frog was observed in its group habitat by 3 observers for five min on Day 14. The observers (who were blind to the experimental condition--they wore headphones over which bullfrog croakings were played to mask the musical condition) counted the number of aggressive acts, the number of jumps, and the length of the longest jump (the starting and landing spots were marked on a sketch of the habitat, and jump length was later converted to distance in meters using a blueprint of the habitat) by the frog being observed.

APA CODES: 3.42–3.49   INDEX NUMBER: 01

NOTES:

Cross-sex pairs of students were placed face-to-face 1.5 ft (0.45 m) apart.

APA CODE: 3.50   INDEX NUMBER: 01

The amount of time it took respondents to blush when embarrassed was 1.4 s.

APA CODE: 3.51   INDEX NUMBER: 01

Rats in the binge-training condition weighed an average of 16 kg; this represented a 600% increase in weight.

APA CODE: 3.51   INDEX NUMBER: 02

Integrative Exercise: Metrication

The alleged ESP signals were transmitted 30 ft (9.1 m) by participants said to possess telepathic power. Participants claiming to have psychokinetic powers attempted to slide a 1.2-kg puck across a 0.001-m line. Those who believed themselves to have precognition ability had to guess the identity of playing cards 10 s before the cards were revealed. Finally, with the participants said to have out-of-body experiences, spiritual transfer was measured in henrys per meter (H/m). Ambient electromagnetic radiation was reduced by placing the participants in a 7-m by 7-m lead cubicle. The lead walls were 1 ft (0.30 m) thick.

APA CODES: 3.50–3.52   INDEX NUMBER: 01

Metrication
APA Codes: 3.50–3.52

These exercises cover APA's policy on metrication, the style for metric units, and metric tables (see the *Publication Manual*, sections 3.50–3.52). Mark corrections directly on the right-hand page and compare your responses with the correct answers on the left-hand page. When you are finished with this section, go on to the next section in which you need practice.

Cross-sex pairs of students were placed face-to-face `1.5 ft` apart.

APA CODE: 3.50   INDEX NUMBER: 01

The amount of time it took respondents to blush when embarrassed was 1.4 `sec`.

APA CODE: 3.51   INDEX NUMBER: 01

Rats in the binge-training condition weighed an average of 16 `K.G.`; this represented a 600% increase in weight.

APA CODE: 3.51   INDEX NUMBER: 02

Integrative Exercise: Metrication

The alleged ESP signals were transmitted 30 ft by participants said to possess telepathic power. Participants claiming to have psychokinetic powers attempted to slide a 1.2-k g puck across a 0.001-m line. Those who believed themselves to have precognition ability had to guess the identity of playing cards 10 secs. before the cards were revealed. Finally, with the participants said to have out-of-body experiences, spiritual transfer was measured in henrys per meter (H/m). Ambient electromagnetic radiation was reduced by placing the participants in a 7-m by 7-m lead cubicle. The lead walls were 1 ft thick.

APA CODES: 3.50–3.52   INDEX NUMBER: 01

NOTES:

A 2 x 2 between-subjects analysis of variance was performed on the judgment scores.

A one-way analysis of variance indicated no effect of the different types of training.

The animals that were raised in a group environment made more social choices (M = 16.8, SD = 1.6) than did the animals that were raised in isolation (M = 10.6, SD = 0.3), $t(38)$ = 4.8, p < .001.

Testing in their native language led to higher scores (M = 84.2, SD = 3.6) than did testing in English (M = 77.4, SD = 2.1), $t(58)$ = 3.7, p < .01.

Table 1 contains the mean number of experiences reported by the respondents in each of the eight groups that composed the 2 x 2 x 2 design. The analysis of variance indicated a significant effect of diary keeping, $F(1, 92)$ = 5.1, p < .01.

The analysis of variance indicated an effect of training style, $F(1, 75)$ = 9.8, p < .001.

Statistical and Mathematical Copy and General Typing Instructions
APA Codes: 3.53–3.61, 5.14

These exercises cover (a) selecting the method of data analysis and retaining data; (b) selecting effective presentation of statistics; (c) references for statistics; (d) formulas; (e) statistics in text; (f) statistical symbols; (g) spacing, alignment, and punctuation; (h) equations in text; and (i) displayed equations (see the *Publication Manual*, sections 3.53–3.61 and 5.14). Mark corrections directly on the right-hand page, and compare your responses with the correct answers on the left-hand page. When you are finished with this section, go on to the next section in which you need practice.

A 2 x 2 between-subjects analysis of variance (Winer, 1971) was performed on the judgment scores.

APA CODE: 3.55   INDEX NUMBER: 01

A one-way analysis of variance $(F = MS_T/MS_E)$ indicated no effect of the different types of training.

APA CODE: 3.56   INDEX NUMBER: 01

The animals that were raised in a group environment made more social choices ($M = 16.8$, $SD = 1.6$) than did the animals that were raised in isolation ($M = 10.6$, $SD = 0.3$), $t_{38} = 4.8$, $p < .001$.

APA CODE: 3.57   INDEX NUMBER: 01

Testing in their native language led to higher scores ($\overline{X} = 84.2$, SD $= 3.6$) than did testing in English ($\overline{X} = 77.4$, SD $= 2.1$), $t(58) = 3.7$, $p < .01$.

APA CODE: 3.57   INDEX NUMBER: 02

Table 1 contains the mean number of experiences reported by the respondents in each of the eight groups that composed the 2 x 2 x 2 design. The analysis of variance indicated a significant effect of diary keeping, $F(1/92) = 5.1$, $p < .01$.

APA CODE: 3.57   INDEX NUMBER: 03

The analysis of variance indicated an effect of training style, $F = 9.8$, df = 1/75, $p < .001$.

APA CODE: 3.57   INDEX NUMBER: 04

There was a significant relation between the task and the sex of the adult partner whom the children chose, $\chi^2(1, N = 58) = 14.78$, $p < .01$.

APA CODE: 3.57   INDEX NUMBER: 05

For increasing drug dosages, the means were 5.6, 4.3, and 1.7, respectively.

APA CODE: 3.58   INDEX NUMBER: 01

The students who agreed to participate (N = 130) were divided into groups according to the severity of their deficiency.

APA CODE: 3.58   INDEX NUMBER: 02

One group of participants (n = 34) received tutorials in the use of the word processing program.

APA CODE: 3.58   INDEX NUMBER: 03

There was a significant relation between the task and the sex of the adult partner whom the children chose, $\chi^2_{1}(58) = 14.78$, $p < .01$.

APA CODE: 3.57   INDEX NUMBER: 05

For increasing drug dosages, $Ms =$ 5.6, 4.3, and 1.7, respectively.

APA CODE: 3.58   INDEX NUMBER: 01

The students who agreed to participate (n = 130) were divided into groups according to the severity of their deficiency.

APA CODE: 3.58   INDEX NUMBER: 02

One group of participants (N = 34) received tutorials in the use of the word processing program.

APA CODE: 3.58   INDEX NUMBER: 03

Integrative Exercise: Statistical and Mathematical Copy and General Typing Instructions

Results

Immediate Testing

Table 1 shows the mean number of aggressive acts and the mean number of jumps during immediate testing for each of the six experimental conditions.

Aggressive behavior. The frogs in the limited-supply conditions engaged in more aggressive behaviors ($M = 3.6$, $SD = 1.2$) than did the frogs in the abundant-supply conditions ($M = 0.8$, $SD = 0.1$). The means for the frogs raised on rock and roll, popular, and classical music were 2.3, 1.9, and 2.4, respectively. A 2 x 3 between-groups analysis of variance confirmed that the effect of food supply was significant, $F(1, 90) = 5.68$, $p < .05$, and that the effect of musical upbringing was not, $F(2, 90) = 1.47$, $p > .20$. The interaction was also not significant ($F < 1$).

Jumping behavior. The frogs in the limited-supply conditions jumped no more frequently ($M = 14.6$, $SD = 4.3$) than did the frogs in the abundant-supply conditions ($M = 14.2$, $SD = 4.1$), $F(1, 90) = 1.24$, $p > .25$. The effect of musical upbringing was highly significant, $F(2, 90) = 16.4$, $p < .001$. The means for the frogs raised on rock and roll, popular, and classical music were 20.5, 13.1, and 9.6, respectively. The interaction was also significant, $F(2, 90) = 5.42$, $p < .01$. As is evident in Table 1, the effect of food supply on jumping was greater for the frogs raised on classical music than for frogs in the other musical conditions. The results for the mean length of the longest jump are not reported, as the effects of the experimental variables were the same for the longest jump as they were for the number of jumps, and the two jumping measures were highly correlated, $r(95) = .89$, $p < .001$.

APA CODES: 3.53–3.61, 5.14   INDEX NUMBER: 01

Integrative Exercise: Statistical and Mathematical Copy and General Typing Instructions

Results

Immediate Testing

Table 1 shows the mean number of aggressive acts and the mean number of jumps during immediate testing for each of the six experimental conditions.

Aggressive behavior. The frogs in the limited-supply conditions engaged in more aggressive behaviors (M = 3.6, SD = 1.2) than did the frogs in the abundant-supply conditions (M = 0.8, SD = 0.1). The Ms for the frogs raised on rock and roll, popular, and classical music were 2.3, 1.9, and 2.4, respectively. A 2 x 3 between-groups analysis of variance confirmed that the effect of food supply was significant, F (1/90) = 5.68, p < 0.05, and that the effect of musical upbringing was not, F (2/90) = 1.47, p > .20. The interaction was also not significant (F < 1).

Jumping behavior. The frogs in the limited-supply conditions jumped no more frequently (14.6, SD = 4.3) than did the frogs in the abundant-supply conditions (14.2, SD = 4.1), F = 1.24, df = 1, 90, p > .25. The effect of musical upbringing was highly significant, F = 16.4, df = 2, 90 p < .001. The means for the frogs raised on rock and roll, popular, and classical music were 20.5, 13.1, and 9.6, respectively. The interaction was also significant, F = 5.42, df = 2, 90, p < .01. As is evident in Table 1, the effect of food supply on jumping was greater for the frogs raised on classical music than for frogs in the other musical conditions. The results for the mean length of the longest jump are not reported, as the effects of the experimental variables were the same for the longest jump as they were for the number of jumps, and the two jumping measures were highly correlated, r(95) = 0.89, p < .001.

APA CODES: 3.53–3.61, 5.14   INDEX NUMBER: 01

NOTES:

Results

Table 1 shows the mean effectiveness ratings of the three types of therapists by the four evaluating groups. A 4 x 3 mixed analysis of variance indicated that the interaction between raters and therapy method was significant, $F(6, 152) = 19.6$, $p < .01$.

APA CODE: 3.62   INDEX NUMBER: 01

- *Note to students:* The feedback frame for this exercise is blank because Table 3 would not exist. The information would be provided more economically in the text of the paper.

APA CODE: 3.62   INDEX NUMBER: 02

Tables and Typing the Parts of a Manuscript
APA Codes: 3.62–3.74, 5.21

These exercises cover tabular versus textual presentation, the relation of tables and text, the relation between tables, table numbers, table title, table headings, the table body, table notes, the ruling of tables, table size, tables from another source, and a table checklist (see the *Publication Manual*, sections 3.62–3.74 and 5.21). Mark corrections directly on the right-hand page, and compare your responses with the correct answers on the left-hand page. When you are finished with this section, take the research report practice test or take one of the research report mastery tests.

Results

The clinical trainers gave mean ratings of effectiveness to the directive, structured, and nondirective therapists of 4.7, 6.2, and 8.7, respectively; the working clinicians assigned ratings of 9.1, 5.3, and 3.6, respectively, to the same therapists; the clinical trainees gave mean ratings of 5.8, 6.6, and 6.4, respectively, to the three groups; and the client sample assigned ratings of 5.9, 3.8, and 1.4, respectively, to the three types of therapists. A 4 x 3 mixed analysis of variance indicated that the interaction between raters and therapy method was significant, $F(6, 152) = 19.6$, $p < .01$.

APA CODE: 3.62   INDEX NUMBER: 01

Table 3

Mean Barking Duration (in Seconds) to Dinner Bell as a Function of Cat's Presence

Cat	M
Absent	33
Present	5

APA CODE: 3.62   INDEX NUMBER: 02

Results

A list of the quantitative modifiers used with the terms *significant* and *nonsignificant* is provided in Table 1. The terms were collected from a sample of articles published in psychological journals in the last 12 years.

APA CODE: 3.63   INDEX NUMBER: 01

Table 2

Mean Time to Write Research Report After Different Kinds of Training and Prior Experience

Prior reports	Type of training			
	None	Lecture	Mastery	Exercises
0	10.4	9.6	7.1	5.3
1	9.1	9.0	6.3	4.1
2	7.4	7.4	5.2	3.8

Note. Times are reported in hours. $n = 20$ in each condition.

- *Note to students:* Other table titles would also suffice, as long as they are brief, identify the independent and dependent variables, and are not redundant with the headings in the table.

APA CODE: 3.66   INDEX NUMBER: 01

Results

A list of the quantitative modifiers used with the terms significant and *nonsignificant* is provided in the table below. The terms were collected from a sample of articles published in psychological journals in the last 12 years.

APA CODE: 3.63   INDEX NUMBER: 01

A Table Listing the Mean Length of Time it Took Participants to Write a Research Report After They Received No Training, Lecture, Mastery Testing, or Exercises and Had Written Either 0, 1, or 2 Prior Reports

| Prior reports | Type of training | | | |
	None	Lecture	Mastery	Exercises
0	10.4	9.6	7.1	5.3
1	9.1	9.0	6.3	4.1
2	7.4	7.4	5.2	3.8

Note. Times are reported in hours. $n = 20$ in each condition.

APA CODE: 3.66   INDEX NUMBER: 01

Table 1

Mean Number of Obstacle Contacts as a Function of Beer Intake and Road Conditions

Road condition	Number of beers				
	0	1	2	4	8
Dry	1	4	5	13	21
Wet	5	9	12	26	41
Icy	11	17	29	34	54

Note. Maximum score = 60. n = 20 per cell.

APA CODE: 3.67   INDEX NUMBER: 01

Table 1

Mean Number of Obstacle Contacts as a Function of Beer Intake and Road Conditions

Condition	0 beers	1 beer	2 beers	4 beers	8 beers
Dry roads	1	4	5	13	21
Wet roads	5	9	12	26	41
Icy roads	11	17	29	34	54

Note. Maximum score = 60. n = 20 per cell.

APA CODE: 3.67   INDEX NUMBER: 01

Table 3

Aggression and Activity in Frogs as a Function of Food Scarcity and Musical Upbringing

Musical heritage	Food supply	
	Limited	Abundant
Aggressive behavior[a]		
Rock and roll	3.8	0.8
Popular	3.4	0.4
Classical	3.6	1.2
Activity level[b]		
Rock and roll	19.7	21.3
Popular	12.7	13.5
Classical	11.4	7.6

Note. $n = 16$ for all cells.

[a]Aggression was measured by number of bumps of another frog.

[b]Activity level was measured by number of jumps.

Correct as is.

APA CODE: 3.67   INDEX NUMBER: 02

Table 3

Aggression and Activity in Frogs as a Function of Food Scarcity and Musical Upbringing

Musical heritage	Food supply	
	Limited	Abundant
	Aggressive behavior[a]	
Rock and roll	3.8	0.8
Popular	3.4	0.4
Classical	3.6	1.2
	Activity level[b]	
Rock and roll	19.7	21.3
Popular	12.7	13.5
Classical	11.4	7.6

Note. n = 16 for all cells.

[a]Aggression was measured by number of bumps of another frog.

[b]Activity level was measured by number of jumps.

APA CODE: 3.67   INDEX NUMBER: 02

Table 6

Effects of Victim Reaction and Social Influence

on Bystander Intervention

	Victim screaming		
Setting	Yes	No	M
Alone	23	17	20
Group	15	9	12
M	19	13	

- *Note to students:* Certainly the row and column totals and means are redundant. Some authors would delete the totals. Ohters would not see a need to include the means either, because the means could be calculated easily by adding the columns or rows and dividing by two.

APA CODE: 3.68   INDEX NUMBER: 01

Table 5

Effects of Anxiety Therapy on Achievement Test Scores

	Test topic	
Therapy	Calculus	History
No treatment	66.4	73.2
Cognitive relaxation	78.8	74.4
Study skills	71.6	82.8
Relaxation and study skills	81.0	36.4

Note. Maximum score = 100. $n = 50$.

Correct as is.

APA CODE: 3.68   INDEX NUMBER: 02

Table 6

Effects of Victim Reaction and Social Influence on Bystander Intervention

Setting	Victim screaming		Total	M
	Yes	No		
Alone	23	17	40	20
Group	15	9	24	12
Total	38	26		
M	19	13		

APA CODE: 3.68   INDEX NUMBER: 01

Table 5

Effects of Anxiety Therapy on Achievement Test Scores

Therapy	Test topic	
	Calculus	History
No treatment	66.4	73.2
Cognitive relaxation	78.8	74.4
Study skills	71.6	82.8
Relaxation and study skills	81.0	36.4

Note. Maximum score = 100. n = 50.

APA CODE: 3.68   INDEX NUMBER: 02

Table 1

Number of Textbook Pages Read for Different Academic Participants in Different Locations

	Study location			
Subject	Dorm	Outdoors	Lounge	Library
Education	4.6	0.8	3.0	6.2
Humanities	9.8	14.1	6.6	33.5
Mathematics	14.2	1.4	3.1	18.4
Science	22.4	3.1	11.0	18.1

Note. Scores are mean number of pages completed. $n = 20$ per cell.

APA CODE: 3.68   INDEX NUMBER: 03

Table 6

Agonistic Behavior of the Weakly Electric Fish

	Social status		
Social behavior	Resident[a]	Intruder[b]	$F(1, 12)$
Chin butt	3.56	0.08	16.68**
Social probe	4.38	1.11	5.57*
Hiding	4.86	10.93	1.88

[a]$n = 4$.   [b]$n = 10$.

*$p < .05$. **$p < .01$.

APA CODE: 3.70   INDEX NUMBER: 01

Table 1

Number of Textbook Pages Read for Different Academic Participants in Different Locations

	Study location			
Subject	Dorm	Outdoors	Lounge	Library
Education	4.6	0.75	3.0	6.2
Humanities	9.8	14.1	6.6	33.50
Mathematics	14.2	1.414	3.1416	18.40
Science	22.4	3.14	11.00	18.12

Note. Scores are mean number of pages completed. $n = 20$ per cell.

APA CODE: 3.68   INDEX NUMBER: 03

Table 6

Agonistic Behavior of the Weakly Electric Fish

	Social status		
Social behavior	Resident[a]	Intruder[b]	$F(1, 12)$
Chin butt	3.56	0.08	16.68**
Social probe	4.38	1.11	5.57*
Hiding	4.86	10.93	1.88

[a]$n = 4$

[b]$n = 10$

NOTE: Two asterisks indicate $p < .01$, one indicates $p < .05$.

APA CODE: 3.70   INDEX NUMBER: 01

Table 17

Job Satisfaction and Quality Circle Participation

	Quality circle program	
Job index	Participants	Nonparticipants
Challenge	5.2	4.5
Accomplishment	5.3	4.6
Meaning	6.2	5.4

APA CODE: 3.71   INDEX NUMBER: 01

Table 17

Job Satisfaction and Quality Circle Participation

	Quality circle program	
Job index	Participants	Nonparticipants
Challenge	5.2	4.5
Accomplishment	5.3	4.6
Meaning	6.2	5.4

APA CODE: 3.71   INDEX NUMBER: 01

Table 4

Mean Imaginal Scores During Different Bodily States of Students Reporting an Out-of-Body Experience (OBE)

	State of consciousness		
Form of OBE	Alert	Daydreaming	Dreaming
Visual			
Abstract	4.7	7.1	5.2
Concrete	3.5	7.4	9.2
Auditory			
Abstract	7.1	4.0	2.2
Concrete	5.5	4.8	1.1
Proprioceptive			
Abstract	3.3	6.9	2.4
Concrete	5.8	7.6	2.7

Note. Scores are based on the mean rating of each student's description by three judges. Cell entries represent mean ratings ($n = 22$).

APA CODE: 5.21   INDEX NUMBER: 01

Table 2

Effects of Distance From Natural Disaster on Relevant Knowledge, Volunteerism, and Anxiety

APA CODE: 5.21   INDEX NUMBER: 02

Table 4

Mean Imaginal Scores During Different Bodily States of Students Reporting an Out-of-Body Experience (OBE)

	State of consciousness		
Form of OBE	Alert	Daydreaming	Dreaming
Visual			
Abstract	4.7	7.1	5.2
Concrete	3.5	7.4	9.2
Auditory			
Abstract	7.1	4.0	2.2
Concrete	5.5	4.8	1.1
Proprioceptive			
Abstract	3.3	6.9	2.4
Concrete	5.8	7.6	2.7

Note. Scores are based on the mean rating of each student's description by three judges. Cell entries represent mean ratings ($n = 22$).

APA CODE: 5.21   INDEX NUMBER: 01

Table 2: Effects of distance from natural disaster on relevant knowledge, volunteerism, and anxiety.

APA CODE: 5.21   INDEX NUMBER: 02

Integrative Exercise: Tables and Typing the Parts of a Manuscript

Table 1

Distribution of Eyewitness Errors During Different Kinds of Interviews After an Actual Murder

	Interviewer	
Error type	Police[a]	Researcher[b]
Actions	53.3	48.5
Descriptions		
People	41.1	34.3
Objects	5.6	17.2

Note. Scores represent the percentage of errors of each type combined over the 11 eyewitnesses. Each eyewitness could make more than one error of each particular type.

[a]Total errors = 107.   [b]Total errors = 198.

- *Note to students:* Other brief titles that specify the independent and dependent variables nonredundantly would also be correct. Furthermore, the arrangement of the table shown above is not the only correct presentation. Depending on the perspective you take in the text, you could have the two different interviewers arranged in the rows and the three different error types arranged in the columns.

APA CODES: 3.62–3.74, 5.21   INDEX NUMBER: 01

Integrative Exercise: Tables and Typing the Parts of a Manuscript

Table 1 *Distribution of Eyewitness Errors About Actions, Descriptions of People, and Descriptions of Objects During Interviews by Police and Researchers After an Actual Murder.*

Error Type	Interviewer
	Police[a]
action	53.271
descriptions	
People	41.121
Objects	5.607
	Researcher[b]
action	48.485
descriptions	
People	34.343
Objects	17.172

Note. Scores represent the percentage of errors of each type combined over the 11 eyewitnesses. Each eyewitness could make more than one error of each particular type. *Footnote*[a]. Total errors = 107. *Footnote*[b]. Total errors = 198.

APA CODES: 3.62–3.74, 5.21   INDEX NUMBER: 01

Research Report Practice Test

The practice test, formatted like the familiarization test, is designed to (a) assess your level of mastery after completing the learning and integrative exercises, (b) help you to decide whether to study particular topics in the *Publication Manual* in more depth, (c) help you to decide whether to go on to the review exercises, and (d) help you to decide whether to take a mastery test. Take this 40-question multiple-choice test. There are two answer sheets at the end of the test, one blank for you to write in your answers and the other containing the correct answers. Beside each blank you will find the APA code that corresponds to the *Publication Manual* section containing the relevant style rule and example. Score your test using the answer key with the correct answers. If you score low (i.e., 80% or lower) on the practice test, we advise you to do the review exercises at the end of the research report unit. If you score above 80%, you may want to take a mastery test, which your instructor will supply.

RESEARCH REPORT PRACTICE TEST

1. A report of an empirical study usually includes an introduction and sections called Method, Results, and

   a. Statistics.
   b. Bibliography.
   c. Discussion.
   d. Statement of the Problem.

2. The abstract of an article should

   a. offer a brief evaluation of the material in the body of the manuscript.
   b. be a concise and specific report on the content of the article.
   c. be written in the passive voice whenever possible.
   d. do all of the above.

3. What question should the introduction section of a research report attempt to answer?

   a. What are the theoretical implications of the current research?
   b. What is the point of the study?
   c. What is the logical link between the problem and the research design?
   d. All of the above are correct.
   e. Only a and c of the above are correct.

4. The Method section should

   a. include enough detail to make replication of the experiment possible for the reader.
   b. briefly describe the method to the reader, omitting details about subjects and apparatus.
   c. fully describe all statistical testing procedures used.
   d. explain why the study was done.

5. In reporting your data

   a. refer to tables of raw data to be exact.
   b. include figures that represent data described fully in the text.
   c. include figures or tables that supplement but are not redundant with data descriptions in the text.
   d. use many figures and tables because they communicate your results best.

6. Tables and figures should

   a. not be referred to in the text.
   b. not be used for data that can be easily presented in a few lines of text.
   c. only be used to represent data that are fully described in the text.
   d. only be used to show inferential statistics.

7. Speculation is in order in the Discussion section when it is

   a. identified as speculation.
   b. logically related to empirical data or the theory being tested.
   c. expressed concisely.
   d. all of the above.
   e. none of the above.

8. What causes the following segment of a student's research report to lack smoothness of expression?

   > According to the research of Savin-Williams (1988), how gay men publicly revealed their sexual orientation is correlated with the stability of their mental health. He finds that well-adjusted gay men reveal early to trusted others.

   a. intransitive inferences
   b. too much jargon
   c. abrupt changes in verb tense
   d. misplaced modifiers

9. When a verb concerns the action of the author-experimenter, the

   a. third person and passive voice should be used.
   b. third person and active voice should be used.
   c. the first person, active voice is used.
   d. third person should be used in all scientific writing to ensure objectivity.

10. Which of the following examples demonstrates correct use of capitalization?

    a. Trial 3 and Item 4
    b. trial *n* and item *x*
    c. chapter 4
    d. Table 2 and Figure 3
    e. All of the above are correct.

11. Edit the following for capitalization:

    > When the hermit crabs listened to classical music, they were significantly more likely to retreat back into their shells than when they listened to rock and roll music. However, there was no music x shell interaction effect.

    a. leave as is
    b. The interaction term *music x shell* should be *Music x Shell*.
    c. Statistical terms such as *significantly* should be capitalized.
    d. *Interaction effect* should be *Interaction Effect*.

12. According to the APA style rules regarding italics,

    a. only Greek letters used as statistical symbols are italicized.

    b. all letters used as statistical symbols except Greek letters should be italicized.

    c. letters used as statistical symbols are never italicized in print.

    d. a and c of the above are correct.

13. Edit the following by selecting the correct arrangement of headings:

Method

Subjects

Procedure

Results

Discussion

    a. leave as is

    b.

Method

Subjects

Procedure

Results

Discussion

    c.

Method

Subjects

Procedure

Results

Discussion

    d.

Method

Subjects

Procedure

Results

Discussion

14. Numerical figures should be used at all times for

    a. ages, times, dates, and percentages.

    b. ratios, arithmetical manipulations, and series of four or more numbers.

    c. fractional or decimal quantities, scores and points on a scale, and units of measurement of time.

    d. all of the above.

15. Edit the following for the expression of numbers:

    It would be wrong to estimate absentees for the week by taking the number of absentees on Monday and multiplying by 5.

    a. leave as is

    b. It would be wrong to estimate absentees for the week by taking the number of absentees on Monday and multiplying by five.

    c. It would be wrong to estimate absentees for the week by taking the number of absentees on Monday and multiplying by five (5).

16. Edit the following for the expression of numbers:

    The authors identify 7 different groups of personality theories.

    a. leave as is

    b. The authors identify seven different groups of personality theories.

    c. Both a and b are correct.

17. Edit the following for the expression of numbers:

    "Large" financial responsibility was defined as responsibility for an annual budget in excess of five million dollars.

    a. leave as is

    b. "Large" financial responsibility was defined as responsibility for an annual budget in excess of $5 x 10^6.

    c. "Large" financial responsibility was defined as responsibility for an annual budget in excess of $5,000,000.

    d. "Large" financial responsibility was defined as responsibility for an annual budget in excess of $5 million.

18. Edit the following for the expression of ordinal numbers:

    The trainees were all in at least their 3rd year of unemployment.

    a. leave as is

    b. The trainees were all in at least their third (3rd) year of unemployment.

    c. The trainees were all in at least their third year of unemployment.

19. When using decimal numbers less than one,

    a. a zero is always used before the decimal point (0.05).
    b. a zero is never used before the decimal point (.05).
    c. the author should check with the editor of each specific journal, as this is a highly controversial topic.
    d. a zero is used before the decimal point (0.05) except when the number cannot be greater than one (e.g., correlations, proportions, and levels of statistical significance; $r = -.96$, $p < .05$).

20. Edit the following for the expression of numbers:

    Days I and IV were baseline days, and Days II and III were treatment days.

    a. leave as is

    b. Days One and Four were baseline days, and Days Two and Three were treatment days.

    c. Days 1 and 4 were baseline days, and Days 2 and 3 were treatment days.

    d. Days I and Four were baseline days, and Days II and III were treatment days.

21. which example is the correct way to use commas and spacing when presenting statistics in text?

    a. $F,(24, 1000)$
    b. $F (24, 1000)$
    c. $F(24, 1000)$
    d. $F (24 1,000)$

22. Which of the following metric units is correctly expressed?

    a. 33 cms.
    b. 3 mm.
    c. 13 cm
    d. 3 cms.

23. Edit the following for the citation of a statistic in text:

    A 4 x 3 analysis of variance (Keppel, 1982) was conducted on the preference scores.

    a. leave as is

    b. A 4 x 3 analysis of variance (see any standard statistics text) was conducted on the preference scores.

    c. A 4 x 3 analysis of variance was conducted on the preference scores.

24. Edit the following for the presentation of formulas:

The relation between premarital sexual experience and incidence of divorce was evaluated using a chi-square test $\{\chi^2 = [\Sigma(\text{Observed} - \text{Expected})/\text{Expected}]\}$.

a. leave as is

b. The relationship between premarital sexual experience and incidence of divorce was evaluated using a chi-square test (see Appendix A for formula).

c. The relationship between premarital sexual experience and incidence of divorce was evaluated using a chi-square test.

25. When presenting statistical information in the text, to clarify the nature of effects (i.e., mean differences and the direction of mean differences),

a. give only the inferential statistics.
b. always give descriptive and inferential statistics.
c. give inferential and descriptive statistics only when presenting correlational data.
d. give inferential statistics for experiments with more than one independent variable and descriptive statistics for correlational research.

26. Edit the following for the use of statistical symbols:

In the group therapy condition, 16 percent of the clients did not return for the second session and another 8 percent did not return for the third session.

a. leave as is

b. In the group therapy condition, 16% of the clients did not return for the second session and another eight percent did not return for the third session.

c. In the group therapy condition, 16% of the clients did not return for the second session and another eight % did not return for the third session.

d. In the group therapy condition, 16% of the clients did not return for the second session and another 8% did not return for the third session.

27. Which of the following should be used to designate the number of cases or observations in a total sample?

a. N
b. N
c. n
d. n

28. Edit Table 17 for errors in tabular presentation and notes to a table:

Table 17

Mean Mood Scores Before and After

Physical Activity

	Mood	
Physical activity	Before	After
Nonaerobic		
Bird watching	3.2	3.7
Bowling	3.0	3.0
Golfing[a]	3.4	2.7
Aerobic		
Cycling	3.3	8.1
Dancing[b]	3.3	8.4
Hill climbing	3.2	8.2
Rowing	3.1	8.0
Running	3.4	7.9
Ski skating	3.1	9.0

Note. Mood was rated on a 10-point scale.

[a]Golfers rode around the course in golf carts. [b]Dancers danced to rock and roll music.

a. The mean values are rounded off too much.
b. There is not enough spacing between columns.
c. The footnotes are in the wrong sequence.
d. Roman numerals should be used to number a table.
e. There are no errors in Table 17.

29. Of the following possible titles for Table 17 (see Question 28), which would not be clear and explanatory?

a. *Mood and Exercise*

b. *Mean Changes in Mood of Subjects Prior to and Following a Variety of Nonaerobic and Aerobic Physical Activities*

c. *A Comparison of Physical Activities*

d. All of the above titles are poorly written.

30. Identify a column spanner in Table 17 (see Question 28):

    a. Bird watching
    b. Cycling
    c. Mood
    d. Aerobic

31. In Table 17 (see Question 28), identify a column heading:

    a. Nonaerobic
    b. Ski skating
    c. Before
    d. Mood

32. A specific note to a table

    a. refers to a particular column or individual entry.
    b. is indicated by a superscript lowercase letter.
    c. is placed below the table.
    d. does all of the above.
    e. does none of the above.

33. Tables, including titles and headings, should be

    a. triple-spaced.
    b. double-spaced.
    c. single-spaced.
    d. any of the above.

34. A good figure

    a. conveys only essential facts.
    b. is easy to understand.
    c. is prepared in the same style as similar figures in the same article.
    d. does all of the above.

35. What kind of graph (a type of figure) is useful to show a continuous change across time?

    a. line
    b. circle
    c. pie
    d. bar
    e. scatter

36. Edit the following for numbering of figures. Assume that this is the first time the figures are presented.

Results

   The predicted social facilitation effects were observed. As can be seen in Figure 2, a videocamera increased errors with the difficult task and decreased errors with the easy task. As can be seen in Figure 1, the presence of an evaluative audience produced the same pattern of results.

    a. leave as is
    b. Figure 2 should be Figure II.
    c. Figure 2 should be Figure Two.
    d. Figure 2 should be Figure 1 and vice versa.

37. Where should figures be placed in a submitted manuscript?

    a. at the end
    b. at the beginning
    c. in an appropriate place in text
    d. None of the above is correct.

38. Edit the following for typing statistical and mathematical copy:

    The students who planned to keep their textbooks wrote on a significantly greater number of their pages (M = 182.4, SD = 6.2) than did the students who planned to sell their textbooks (M = 128.6, SD = 1.7), $t($ 46 $)$ = 3.27, $p<.01$.

    a. leave as is

    b. The students who planned to keep their textbooks wrote on a significantly greater number of their pages (M = 182.4, SD = 6.2) than did the students who planned to sell their textbooks (M = 128.6, SD = 1.7), $t(46)$ = 3.27, $p < .01$.

    c. The students who planned to keep their textbooks wrote on a significantly greater number of their pages (M = 182.4, SD = 6.2) than did the students who planned to sell their textbooks (M = 128.6, SD = 1.7), $t(46)$ = $3.27,p<.01$.

    d. The students who planned to keep their textbooks wrote on a significantly greater number of their pages (M = 182.4, SD = 6.2) than did the students who planned to sell their textbooks (M = 128.6, SD = 1.7), t (46) = 3.27, $p<.01$.

39. A running head to be used in a research report should be typed

    a. centered at the bottom of the title page in all uppercase letters.
    b. flush left at the top of the title page.
    c. centered at the bottom of the title page in uppercase and lowercase letters.
    d. flush right at the bottom of the title page.

40. In the text of a manuscript, cite each table by

    a. writing instructions in the margin.
    b. putting a clear break in the text with the instruction "Insert Table ___ about here" set off by lines above and below.
    c. typing instructions in brackets.
    d. using the word *Table* and an arabic numeral.

RESEARCH REPORT PRACTICE TEST
ANSWER SHEET AND FEEDBACK REPORT

Student Name _____ **Date** _____

Question Number	Answer	APA Codes	Question Number	Answer	APA Codes
1	_____	1.01–1.04	21	_____	3.42–3.49
2	_____	1.06–1.07	22	_____	3.50–3.52
3	_____	1.08–1.09	23	_____	3.53–3.59
4	_____	1.08–1.09	24	_____	3.53–3.59
5	_____	1.10–1.13	25	_____	3.53–3.59
6	_____	1.10–1.13	26	_____	3.53–3.59
7	_____	1.10–1.13	27	_____	3.53–3.59
8	_____	2.01–2.02	28	_____	3.62–3.72
9	_____	2.03–2.05	29	_____	3.62–3.72
10	_____	3.12–3.18	30	_____	3.62–3.72
11	_____	3.12–3.18	31	_____	3.62–3.72
12	_____	3.19	32	_____	3.62–3.72
13	_____	3.30–3.33	33	_____	3.74
14	_____	3.42–3.49	34	_____	3.75–3.81
15	_____	3.42–3.49	35	_____	3.75–3.81
16	_____	3.42–3.49	36	_____	3.83–3.84
17	_____	3.42–3.49	37	_____	5.01–5.08
18	_____	3.42–3.49	38	_____	5.09–5.14
19	_____	3.42–3.49	39	_____	5.15–5.25
20	_____	3.42–3.49	40	_____	5.15–5.25

NUMBER CORRECT _____

RESEARCH REPORT PRACTICE TEST
ANSWER KEY

Question Number	Answer	APA Codes	Question Number	Answer	APA Codes
1	c	1.01–1.04	21	c	3.42–3.49
2	b	1.06–1.07	22	c	3.50–3.52
3	d	1.08–1.09	23	c	3.53–3.59
4	a	1.08–1.09	24	c	3.53–3.59
5	c	1.10–1.13	25	b	3.53–3.59
6	b	1.10–1.13	26	d	3.53–3.59
7	d	1.10–1.13	27	a	3.53–3.59
8	c	2.01–2.02	28	e	3.62–3.72
9	c	2.03–2.05	29	d	3.62–3.72
10	e	3.12–3.18	30	c	3.62–3.72
11	b	3.12–3.18	31	c	3.62–3.72
12	b	3.19	32	d	3.62–3.72
13	b	3.30–3.33	33	b	3.74
14	d	3.42–3.49	34	d	3.75–3.81
15	a	3.42–3.49	35	a	3.75–3.81
16	b	3.42–3.49	36	d	3.83–3.84
17	d	3.42–3.49	37	a	5.01–5.08
18	a	3.42–3.49	38	b	5.09–5.14
19	d	3.42–3.49	39	b	5.15–5.25
20	c	3.42–3.49	40	d	5.15–5.25

Research Report Review Exercises

NOTES:

Review Exercise: Capitalization and General Typing Instructions

In their article "Work That Works Groups: Performance Enhancement With Disjunctive Tasks," Blaine and Walker (1989) concluded that groups can appear to do better than individuals when tasks allow disjunctive problem-solving processes. However, with conjunctive tasks, individuals appear to perform better than groups. Because there was a Group Size x Task interaction, selection of only one task yielded results that favored either social loafing theory or assembly bonus theory.

To test their hypothesis, we compared the performance of individuals assigned with either a conjunctive task condition or a disjunctive task condition. The expected results of Trials 1, 2, and 3 are displayed in Figure 1.

APA CODES: 3.12–3.18, 5.09   INDEX NUMBER: 02

Research Report Review Exercises

Review exercises are all in the integrative format and cover the same topics as the learning exercises and integrative exercises. The components in need of correction are not shaded, but the errors in each review exercise are all related to the style rules contained in a specific part of the *Publication Manual* (e.g., tables, metrication). Read the text carefully and edit the text, marking corrections directly on the draft version. The corrections on the feedback page are shaded. Review exercises are designed to give you additional practice, to help you review style points you have already studied, and to further prepare you to take a mastery test.

Review Exercise: Capitalization and General Typing Instructions

In their article "Work that works groups: Performance enhancement with disjunctive tasks," Blaine and Walker (1989) concluded that groups can appear to do better than individuals when tasks allow disjunctive problem-solving processes. However, with Conjunctive Tasks, individuals appear to perform better than groups. Because there was a group size X task interaction, selection of only one task yielded results that favored either Social Loafing theory or Assembly Bonus Theory.

To test their hypothesis, we compared the performance of individuals assigned with either a Conjunctive Task Condition or a Disjunctive Task Condition. The expected results of trials 1, 2, and 3 are displayed in figure 1.

APA CODES: 3.12–3.18, 5.09   INDEX NUMBER: 02

Review Exercise: Abbreviations

After being randomly assigned to groups, the paramedical staff began 9 weeks of team building (e.g., fishbowling, disaster simulations, role playing, etc.). Subsequently, each staff member was reassigned to a delivery-of-assistance (DOA) unit. One week passed, and all members of the DOA units received 3 weeks of rational emotive therapy (RET). Finally, a 3-hr evaluation of each DOA unit was conducted by an international team of health care experts assigned by the United Nations (UN). In one part of the speeded-disaster simulation, the unit was given 48 s to extricate a robot victim from a burning car. An independent observer kept track of the distance between each staff member and the car in meters.

APA CODES: 3.20–3.29   INDEX NUMBER: 02

Review Exercise: Abbreviations

After being randomly assigned to groups, the paramedical staff began 9 wks of team building eg, fishbowling, disaster simulations, role playing, etc. Subsequently, each staff member was reassigned to a delivery-of-assistance (DOA) unit. One week passed, and all members of the delivery-of-assistance (DOA) units received 3 weeks of rational emotive therapy (R.E.T.). Finally, a 3-hr evaluation of each delivery-of-assistance unit was conducted by an international team of health care experts assigned by the United Nations (U.N.). In one part of the speeded-disaster simulation, the unit was given 48 seconds to extricate a robot victim from a burning car. An independent observer kept track of the distance between each staff member and the car in m.

APA CODES: 3.20–3.29   INDEX NUMBER: 02

Method

Participants

The participants were 228 students from an introductory psychology course who volunteered to attend an extra lecture of the course.

Design

The investigation included two predictor variables and one manipulated variable. One predictor variable, sex of the student, was dichotomous; the other predictor variable, student's score on Exam 1 of the course, was treated as a continuous variable. The manipulated variable was method of delivery of the lecture.

Procedure

Recruitment of participants. During the second unit of the course, which followed Exam 1, the major topic was learning and behavior control. The students were invited to attend an extra lecture, outside of the regularly scheduled class time. The instructor told the students that (a) they could sign up for any of a variety of times, (b) the lecture would be presented on videotape, (c) the lecture would describe applications of behavior-modification techniques to clinical and personal problems, (d) the material was optional and would not be tested directly on the next exam, and (e) the discussion of the applications would probably help the students understand the basic principles that would be covered on the next exam.

(*continued*)

Method

Participants

The participants were 228 students from an introductory psychology course who volunteered to attend an extra lecture of the course.

Design

The investigation included two predictor variables and one manipulated variable. One predictor variable, sex of the student, was dichotomous; the other predictor variable, student's score on Exam 1 of the course, was treated as a continuous variable. The manipulated variable was method of delivery of the lecture.

Procedure

Recruitment of Participants

During the second unit of the course, which followed Exam 1, the major topic was learning and behavior control. The students were invited to attend an extra lecture, outside of the regularly scheduled class time. The instructor told the students that *a:* they could sign up for any of a variety of times, *b:* the lecture would be presented on videotape, *c:* the lecture would describe applications of behavior-modification techniques to clinical and personal problems, *d:* the material was optional and would not be tested directly on the next exam, and *e:* the discussion of the applications would probably help the students understand the basic principles that would be covered on the next exam.

(*continued*)

Manipulation of lecture delivery. Three videotapes were made of the instructor delivering the identical lecture: (a) reading, for which the instructor kept her head down to read the entire lecture, making eye contact with the camera only rarely; (b) using notes, for which the instructor glanced down frequently but also made occasional eye contact with the camera; and (c) from memory, for which the instructor had no notes and made frequent eye contact with the camera. The instructor was dressed the same and said the identical words on all three tapes. Students viewed the videotapes in groups of 4-8 students each. Tapes were assigned to groups randomly, with an attempt to equalize the number of students who received each form of delivery.

Predictor variables. At the end of the videotape, the purpose of the investigation was explained to the students. They were each given a card on which to record their sex and their score on Exam 1 (a list of students and exam scores was available for the students to check their own scores).

Dependent measures. The experimenter, who showed the videotape, then recorded on each student's card the number of lines on which the student had written notes (as the measure of amount of notes) and the number of indentation shifts in the student's notes (as the measure of organization of notes).

Results

APA CODES: 3.30–3.33, 5.10, 5.12   INDEX NUMBER: 02

Manipulation of Lecture Delivery

Three videotapes were made of the instructor delivering the identical lecture: (1) reading, for which the instructor kept her head down to read the entire lecture, making eye contact with the camera only rarely, (2) using notes, for which the instructor glanced down frequently but also made occasional eye contact with the camera, and (3) from memory, for which the instructor had no notes and made frequent eye contact with the camera. The instructor was dressed the same and said the identical words on all three tapes. Students viewed the videotapes in groups of 4-8 students each. Tapes were assigned to groups randomly, with an attempt to equalize the number of students who received each form of delivery.

Predictor Variables

At the end of the videotape, the purpose of the investigation was explained to the students. They were each given a card on which to record their sex and their score on Exam 1 (a list of students and exam scores was available for the students to check their own scores).

Dependent Measures

The experimenter, who showed the videotape, then recorded on each student's card the number of lines on which the student had written notes (as the measure of amount of notes) and the number of indentation shifts in the student's notes (as the measure of organization of notes).

Results

APA CODES: 3.30–3.33, 5.10, 5.12   INDEX NUMBER: 02

Review Exercise: Numbers

The 60 studies published in the last 20 years (1969-1988) that reported evaluations of treatments for extreme fear reactions to a specific fictional character from a book, TV, or film (monstrophobia) were reviewed, and a meta-analysis of the results was performed.

The participants in the different studies were male and female individuals ranging in age from 3 to 96 years old who had reported a phobic reaction to at least one character. As assessed by self-report (in 40 of the studies), the mean duration of exposure to the character prior to development of the phobic reaction was 4 min. The participants in 37 of the studies reported a phobic reaction to only one character; the participants in 12 of the studies reported a phobic reaction to two characters; the participants in 7 of the studies reported a phobic reaction to one or two characters; and the participants in the remaining 4 studies reported a reaction to as few as one character and as many as seven different characters. There were nine different characters reported as phobic objects by 1 or more clients in the different studies: the Wicked Witch of the East, the Wicked Witch of the West, the Phantom of the Opera, Dr. Frankenstein, Dr. Frankenstein's Monster, Medusa, the Big Bad Wolf, Jaws, and Cookie Monster. Twenty-eight of the studies (including 823 participants) reported data on the number of additional phobias (other than monstrophobia) reported by the participants; on the basis of those data, the mean number of additional phobias was 0.16.

(continued)

Review Exercise: Numbers

The sixty studies published in the last twenty years (1969-1988) that reported evaluations of treatments for extreme fear reactions to a specific fictional character from a book, TV, or film (monstrophobia) were reviewed, and a meta-analysis of the results was performed.

The participants in the different studies were male and female individuals ranging in age from three to 96 years old who had reported a phobic reaction to at least 1 character. As assessed by self-report (in 40 of the studies), the mean duration of exposure to the character prior to development of the phobic reaction was 4 min. The participants in 37 of the studies reported a phobic reaction to only 1 character; the participants in 12 of the studies reported a phobic reaction to two characters; the participants in seven of the studies reported a phobic reaction to one or two characters; and the participants in the remaining four studies reported a reaction to as few as one character and as many as seven different characters. There were nine different characters reported as phobic objects by 1 or more clients in the different studies: the Wicked Witch of the East, the Wicked Witch of the West, the Phantom of the Opera, Dr. Frankenstein, Dr. Frankenstein's Monster, Medusa, the Big Bad Wolf, Jaws, and Cookie Monster. 28 of the studies (including 823 participants) reported data on the number of additional phobias (other than monstrophobia) reported by the participants; on the basis of those data, the mean number of additional phobias was .16.

(continued)

Studies were included in the evaluation if they compared a treatment with a no-treatment control or with at least one other treatment. In actuality, the different studies assessed 1, 2, 3, or 6 different treatment methods. Treatments lasted from 1 day to 6 months and from 1 to 50 sessions. Participants were treated individually or in groups of up to 8 participants per group. The sample sizes for a given treatment ranged from 1 to 24 in the individual studies. Combining all of the studies, the number of participants who received each treatment ranged from 14 to 238, and the total number of participants was 1,942.

The 60 studies are listed in Table 1, with an indication of which of eight different treatments (two behavioral methods [desensitization and flooding], cognitive therapy, rational therapy, client-centered therapy, psychodynamic therapy, hypnosis, and a form of eclectic talk therapy) were assessed in the study, the sample size for each treatment, and the duration of each treatment. Overall, the correlation between number of phobic characters and treatment effectiveness was −.38, and the correlation between number of sessions and treatment effectiveness was .46.

APA CODES: 3.42–3.49   INDEX NUMBER: 02

Review Exercise: Metrication

To determine two-point thresholds, point distance and point pressure were varied. Point distance was measured in millimeters and pressure was measured in grams. The lower lips of subjects were taped to a 2-cm by 3-cm plastic restrainer. Some male orangutans required slightly larger restrainers. Pictures and words were then presented to the orangutans with the lowest thresholds. Pictures were 3 ft (0.91 m) high and 4 ft (1.21 m) long. Words were 2 m high and 4 m long. Identification reaction time was recorded in milliseconds.

APA CODES: 3.50–3.52   INDEX NUMBER: 02

Studies were included in the evaluation if they compared a treatment with a no-treatment control or with at least one other treatment. In actuality, the different studies assessed one, two, three, or six different treatment methods. Treatments lasted from one day to six months and from 1 to 50 sessions. Participants were treated individually or in groups of up to eight participants per group. The sample sizes for a given treatment ranged from 1 to 24 in the individual studies. Combining all of the studies, the number of participants who received each treatment ranged from 14 to 238, and the total number of participants was 1942.

The 60 studies are listed in Table I, with an indication of which of 8 different treatments (2 behavioral methods [desensitization and flooding], cognitive therapy, rational therapy, client-centered therapy, psychodynamic therapy, hypnosis, and a form of eclectic talk therapy) were assessed in the study, the sample size for each treatment, and the duration of each treatment. Overall, the correlation between number of phobic characters and treatment effectiveness was -0.38, and the correlation between number of sessions and treatment effectiveness was $+0.46$.

APA CODES: 3.42–3.49   INDEX NUMBER: 02

Review Exercise: Metrication

To determine two-point thresholds, point distance and point pressure were varied. Point distance was measured in mms and pressure was measured in grams. The lower lips of subjects were taped to a 2- by 3-centimeter plastic restrainer. Some male orangutans required slightly larger restrainers. Pictures and words were then presented to the orangutans with the lowest thresholds. Pictures were 3 feet high and 4 feet long. Words were 2 m high and 4 m long. Identification reaction time was recorded in milliseconds.

APA CODES: 3.50–3.52   INDEX NUMBER: 02

Results and Discussion

As expected, green and red chicks could identify themselves after self-familiarity training. Chicks raised alone in mirrored chambers, when presented with pictures of themselves and opposite-colored strangers, pecked pictures of strangers (M = 11, SD = 2.4) more often than they pecked pictures of themselves (M = 2, SD = 0.5), $t(38)$ = 2.05, p < .05. When put in the actual company of strange chicks, self-familiar chicks pecked strangers a mean of 12 times, the same as did chicks that did not receive self-familiarity training. However, the similarity of the stranger affected the chicks that received familiarity training more than it did the chicks that did not receive training. Self-familiar chicks pecked opposite-colored strangers (M = 16, SD = 5.2) more often than did chicks that did not receive self-familiarity training (M = 13, SD = 3.0), whereas self-familiar chicks pecked same-colored strangers (M = 8, SD = 1.8) less often than did chicks that did not receive self-familiarity training (M = 11, SD = 2.4). The pecking pattern produced a significant interaction between self-familiarity and similarity, $F(1, 38)$ = 8.2, p < .01.

Review Exercise: Statistical and Mathematical Copy and Typing the Parts of a Manuscript

Results and Discussion

As expected, green and red chicks could identify themselves after self-familiarity training. Chicks raised alone in mirrored chambers, when presented with pictures of themselves and opposite-colored strangers, pecked pictures of strangers (mean = 11, standard deviation = 2.4) more often than they pecked pictures of themselves (mean = 2, standard deviation = 0.5), $t(38) = 2.05$, $p < .05$. When put in the actual company of strange chicks, self-familiar chicks pecked strangers a M of 12 times, the same as did chicks that did not receive self-familiarity training. However, the similarity of the stranger affected the chicks that received familiarity training more than it did the chicks that did not receive training. Self-familiar chicks pecked opposite-colored strangers ($M = 16$, $SD = 5.2$) more often than did chicks that did not receive self-familiarity training ($M = 13$, $SD = 3.0$), whereas self-familiar chicks pecked same-colored strangers ($M = 8$, $SD = 1.8$) less often than did chicks that did not receive self-familiarity training ($M = 11$, $SD = 2.4$). The pecking pattern produced a significant interaction between self-familiarity and similarity, F ($df = 1/38$) = 8.2, $p < .01$. Calculations of means and t statistics were done according to procedures described in Ferguson (1988).

APA CODES: 3.53–3.61, 5.14   INDEX NUMBER: 02

Review Exercise: Tables and Typing the Parts of a Manuscript

Table 2

Discrimination Between Recently Mated and Unmated Male Hamsters by Female Hamsters With Different Sexual Experiences

	Male's experience		
Female group[a]	Mated	Unmated	p[b]
Sexually naive	716	862	.05
Sexually experienced (no pretest copulation)	719	903	.05
Sexually experienced (pretest copulation)	536	1,031	.001

Note. The males were anesthetized but the females were not. Scores represent the mean time (in seconds) spent with a male.

[a]There were 28 females in each group. [b]Wilcoxon signed-ranks tests were used.

APA CODES: 3.62–3.74, 5.21   INDEX NUMBER: 02–03

Review Exercise: Tables and Typing the Parts of a Manuscript

Table 2: *Discrimination between recently mated and unmated male hamsters by female hamsters with different sexual experiences*

FEMALE GROUP[a]	MALE'S EXPERIENCE		
	Yes	No	p[b]
Sexually Naive	716.25	862	.05
Had Sexual Experience (no pretest copulation)	719.0	903	.05
No Sexual Experience (pretest copulation)	535.67	1031	.001

[a]There were 28 females in each group.

[b]Wilcoxon signed-ranks tests were used.

Note: The males were anesthetized but the females were not. Scores represent the mean time (in seconds) spent with a male.

APA CODES: 3.62–3.74, 5.21   INDEX NUMBER: 02–03

Research Report Mastery Tests

The *Instructor's Resource Guide* contains four mastery tests for each unit (term paper and research report). Your instructor will decide whether to give you one or more mastery tests as a means of evaluating your knowledge of APA style and your readiness to prepare writing assignments. These tests are similar in structure and content to the familiarization and practice tests but contain different questions. Your instructor will provide you with the mastery tests and may or may not grade them; a grade is useful only for demonstrating that you have mastered APA style (90% correct is the standard for mastery unless your instructor announces otherwise).

Like the familiarization and practice tests, the mastery tests contain 40 multiple-choice questions, along with the APA codes indicating where in the *Publication Manual* you can find the answers. However, you may not use the *Publication Manual* as you take the tests. Your instructor will give you a grade and feedback about any areas in which you need further work.